THE BEST GUITAR SONGBOOK EVER

SUEDE
Animal Nitrate 4
Beautiful Ones 6

KULA SHAKER
Hey Dude 9
Tattva 12

BOYZONE
Baby Can I Hold You? 14

THE CRANBERRIES
Dreams 16

METALLICA
Enter Sandman 18
Fade To Black 20

THE CORRS
Forgiven, Not Forgotten 22
What Can I Do? 24

THE JAM
That's Entertainment 27
The Bitterest Pill (I Ever Had To Swallow) 30
The Eton Rifles 33

THE STONE ROSES
Love Spreads 36

THE LEVELLERS
One Way 38

PAUL WELLER
Sunflower 40

ERIC CLAPTON
Layla 42
Sunshine Of Your Love 44
Tears In Heaven 46

Playing Guide:
Relative Tuning/Reading Chord Boxes 3

This publication is not authorised for sale in the United States of America and/or Canada.

Wise Publications
London/New York/Paris/Sydney/Copenhagen/Madrid

Exclusive distributors:
Music Sales Limited
8/9 Frith Street,
London W1V 5TZ, England.
Music Sales Pty Limited
120 Rothschild Avenue
Rosebery, NSW 2018,
Australia.

Order No.AM956142
ISBN 0-7119-7760-7
This book © Copyright 1999 by Wise Publications
www.internetmusicshop.com

Unauthorised reproduction of any part of this publication by any means including photocopying is an infringement of copyright.

Book design by Chloë Alexander
Photographs courtesy of London Features International

Printed in the United Kingdom by
Caligraving Limited, Thetford, Norfolk.

Your Guarantee of Quality
As publishers, we strive to produce every book to the highest commercial standards. The music has been freshly engraved and book has been carefully designed to minimise awkward page turns and to make playing from it a real pleasure. Particular care has been given to specifying acid-free, neutral-sized paper made from pulps which have not been elemental chlorine bleached. This pulp is from farmed sustainable forests and was produced with special regard for the environment. Throughout, the printing and binding have been planned to ensure a sturdy, attractive publication which should give years of enjoyment. If your copy fails to meet our high standards, please inform us and we will gladly replace it.

Music Sales' complete catalogue describes thousands of titles and is available in full colour sections by subject, direct from Music Sales Limited. Please state your areas of interest and send a cheque/postal order for £1.50 for postage to: Music Sales Limited, Newmarket Road, Bury St. Edmunds, Suffolk IP33 3YB.

Relative Tuning

The guitar can be tuned with the aid of pitch pipes or dedicated electronic guitar tuners which are available through your local music dealer. If you do not have a tuning device, you can use relative tuning. Estimate the pitch of the 6th string as near as possible to E or at least a comfortable pitch (not too high, as you might break other strings in tuning up). Then, while checking the various positions on the diagram, place a finger from your left hand on the:

5th fret of the E or 6th string and **tune the open A** (or 5th string) to the note (A)

5th fret of the A or 5th string and **tune the open D** (or 4th string) to the note (D)

5th fret of the D or 4th string and **tune the open G** (or 3rd string) to the note (G)

4th fret of the G or 3rd string and **tune the open B** (or 2nd string) to the note (B)

5th fret of the B or 2nd string and **tune the open E** (or 1st string) to the note (E)

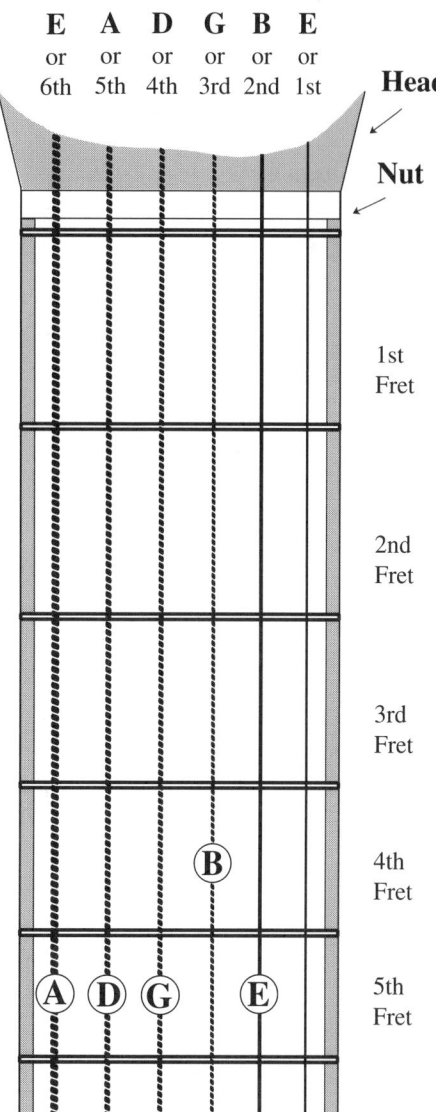

Reading Chord Boxes

Chord boxes are diagrams of the guitar neck viewed head upwards, face on as illustrated. The top horizontal line is the nut, unless a higher fret number is indicated, the others are the frets.

The vertical lines are the strings, starting from E (or 6th) on the left to E (or 1st) on the right.

The black dots indicate where to place your fingers.

Strings marked with an O are played open, not fretted.

Strings marked with an X should not be played.

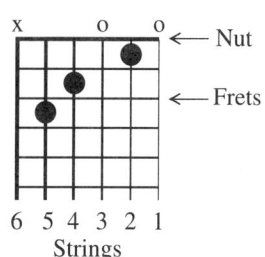

ANIMAL NITRATE

Words & Music by Brett Anderson & Bernard Butler

Bsus2   Bm   A*   Asus4   G*   G5alt   G5
Em   G   A   D   F5   C5   G#

Tune guitar down one semitone

Intro
| Bsus2 Bm Bsus2 A* Asus4 A* | G* G5alt G5 Em |

‖: Bm   A* Asus4 A* | G   Em :‖ *Play 3 times*

Verse 1
      Bm A   G   Em
Like his dad you know that he's had
Bm   A   G   Em
Animal nitrate in mind.
           Bm   A   G   Em
Oh, in your council home he jumped on your bones,
        Bm   A   G
Now you're taking it time after time.

Chorus 1
       A   D   G D   G
Oh, it turns you on, ___ on, ___
Bm   A   G
And now he has gone.
        A   D   G D   G
Oh, what turns you on, ___ on, ___
Bm   A   F5   C5
Now your animal's gone? ___

Verse 1
      Bm A   G   Em
Well he said he'd show you his bed
          Bm   A   G   Em
And the delights of the chemical smile, ___
         Bm   A   G   Em
So in your broken home he broke all your bones,
        Bm   A   G
Now you're taking it time after time.

© Copyright 1992 PolyGram Music Publishing Limited, 47 British Grove, London W4.
All Rights Reserved. International Copyright Secured.

Chorus 2

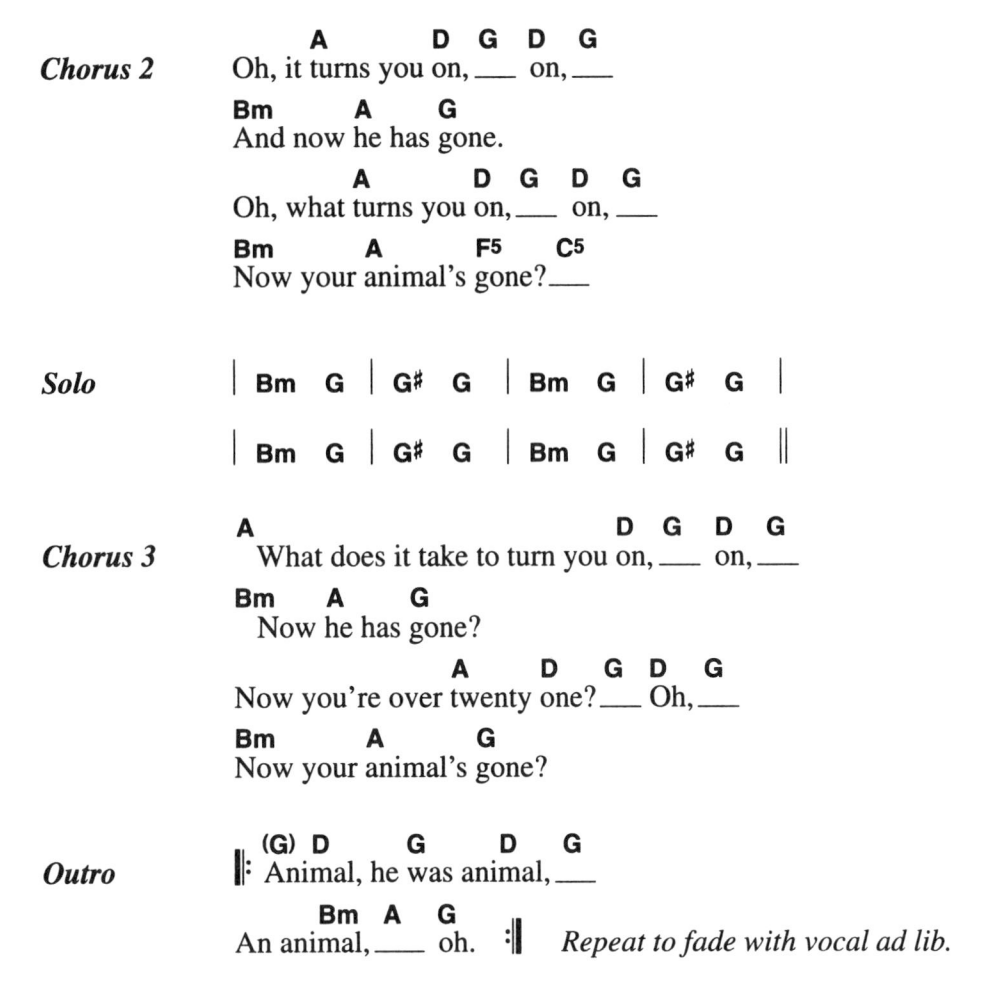

        A   **D G D G**
Oh, it turns you on, ___ on, ___

Bm   **A**   **G**
And now he has gone.

          A   **D G D G**
Oh, what turns you on, ___ on, ___

Bm   **A**   **F5**   **C5**
Now your animal's gone? ___

Solo

| Bm G | G# G | Bm G | G# G |

| Bm G | G# G | Bm G | G# G ||

Chorus 3

A   **D G D G**
  What does it take to turn you on, ___ on, ___

Bm   **A**   **G**
  Now he has gone?

                   A   **D G D G**
Now you're over twenty one? ___ Oh, ___

Bm   **A**   **G**
Now your animal's gone?

Outro

    (G) D   **G**   **D**   **G**
||: Animal, he was animal, ___

        Bm **A**   **G**
An animal, ___ oh. :|| *Repeat to fade with vocal ad lib.*

BEAUTIFUL ONES

Words & Music by Brett Anderson & Richard Oakes

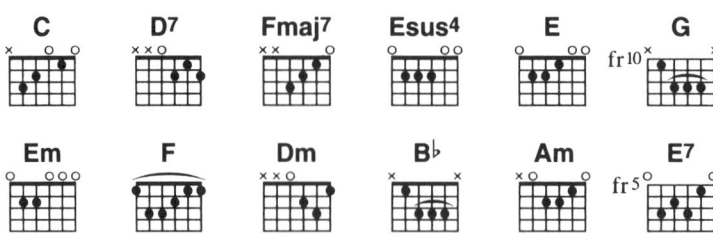

Tune guitar down one semitone

Intro ‖: C | D7 | Fmaj7 | Esus4 E :‖

Verse 1
      C   D7
Ooh, high on diesel and gasoline,
       Fmaj7
Psycho for drum machine,
         Esus4   E
Shaking their bits to the hits, oh.
C   D7
Drag acts, drug acts, suicides,
      Fmaj7
In your dad's suit you hide,
    Esus4 E
Staining his name again, oh.

Verse 2
    C   D7
Cracked up, stacked up, twenty-two,
     Fmaj7
Psycho for sex and glue,
   Esus4 E
Lost it in Bostik, yeah.
C   D7
Oh, shaved heads, rave heads, on the pill,
     Fmaj7
Got too much time to kill,
   E   G
Get into the bands and gangs, oh.

© Copyright 1996 PolyGram Music Publishing Limited, 47 British Grove, London W4.
All Rights Reserved. International Copyright Secured.

Chorus 1

    C
Here they come,
        Em
The beautiful ones,
      F
The beautiful ones,
Dm   **B♭**
La la la la.
C
Here they come,
        Em
The beautiful ones,
      F
The beautiful ones,
Dm   **B♭** **Am** **E7**
La la la la la, la la.

Verse 3

    C   **D7**
Loved up, doved up, hung around,
          Fmaj7
Stoned in a lonely town,
           Esus4   **E**
Shaking their meat to the beat, oh.
C   **D7**
High on diesel and gasoline,
       Fmaj7
Psycho for drum machine,
          Esus4   **E** **G**
Shaking their bits to the hits, oh.

Chorus 2

C
Here they come,
  Em
The beautiful ones,
  F
The beautiful ones,
Dm **B♭**
La la la la.
C
Here they come,
  Em
The beautiful ones,
  F   **Dm**
The beautiful ones, oh oh.

Bridge

    B♭   **C**
  You don't think about it,
          Em
You don't do without it,
          F   **Dm**
Because you're beautiful, yeah, yeah.
B♭   **C**   **Em**
  And if your baby's going crazy,
          F   **Dm**
That's how you made me, la la.
B♭   **C**   **Em**
  And if your baby's going crazy,
          F   **Dm**
That's how you made me, woah woah,
B♭   **C**   **Em**
  And if your baby's going crazy,
          F
That's how you made me,
Dm **B♭** **Am** **E7**
La la, la la, la. La, la.

Outro

   C   **D7**
𝄆 La la la la, la,
         Fmaj7
La la la la la, la.
         Esus4
La la la la la la,
   E
La la la, oh. 𝄇 *Repeat to fade*

HEY DUDE

Words & Music by Crispian Mills, Alonza Bevan, Paul Winter-Hart & Jay Darlington

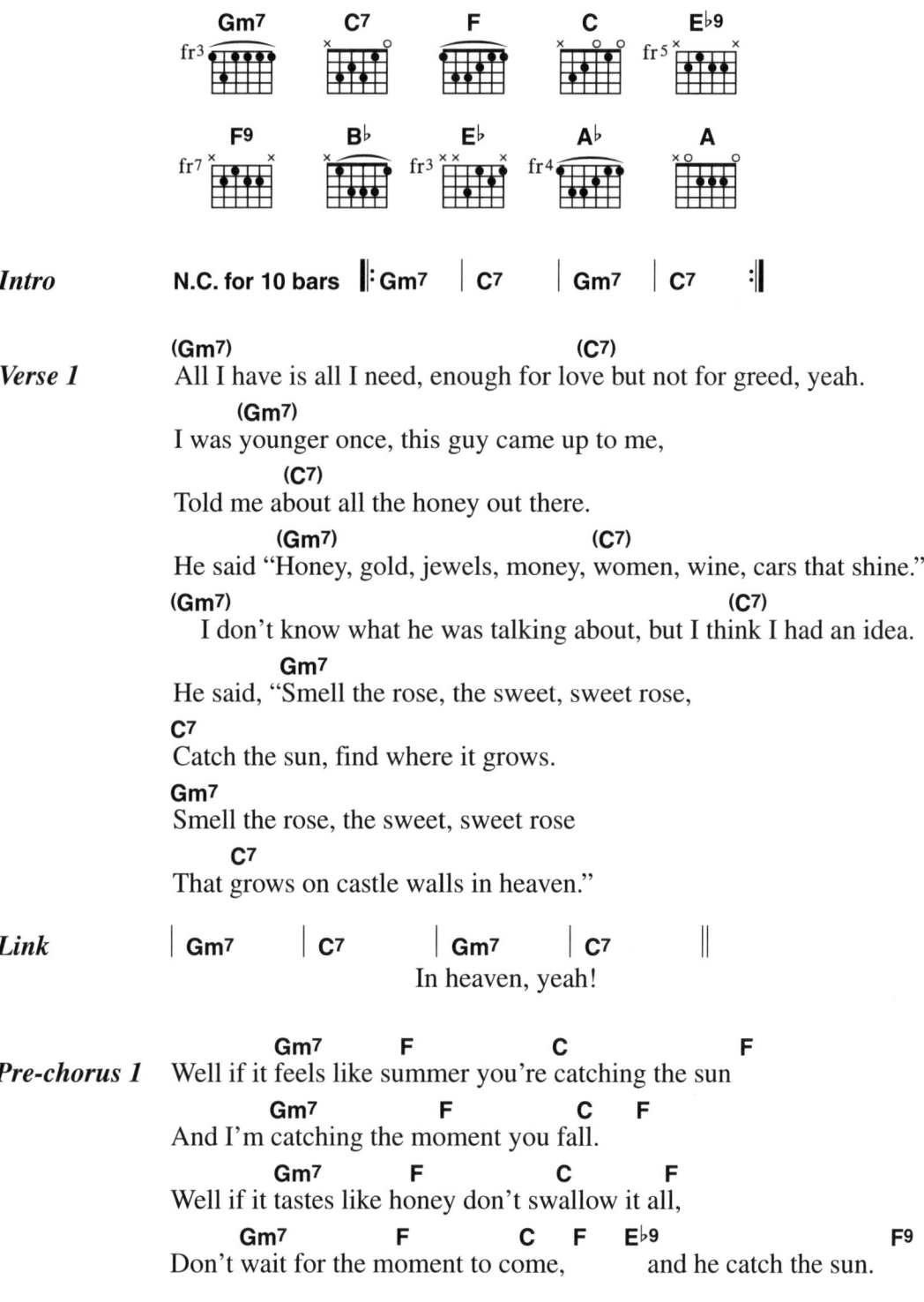

Intro   N.C. for 10 bars ‖: Gm7 | C7 | Gm7 | C7 :‖

Verse 1
         (Gm7)   (C7)
         All I have is all I need, enough for love but not for greed, yeah.
             (Gm7)
         I was younger once, this guy came up to me,
                (C7)
         Told me about all the honey out there.
                (Gm7)   (C7)
         He said "Honey, gold, jewels, money, women, wine, cars that shine."
         (Gm7)   (C7)
            I don't know what he was talking about, but I think I had an idea.
                    Gm7
         He said, "Smell the rose, the sweet, sweet rose,
         C7
         Catch the sun, find where it grows.
         Gm7
         Smell the rose, the sweet, sweet rose
                 C7
         That grows on castle walls in heaven."

Link | Gm7 | C7 | Gm7 | C7   ‖
                          In heaven, yeah!

                   Gm7   F   C   F
Pre-chorus 1 Well if it feels like summer you're catching the sun
                    Gm7   F   C   F
              And I'm catching the moment you fall.
                      Gm7   F   C   F
              Well if it tastes like honey don't swallow it all,
                    Gm7   F   C   F   Eb9   F9
              Don't wait for the moment to come,   and he catch the sun.

© Copyright 1995 Hoodoo Music Limited/Hit & Run Music (Publishing) Limited, 30 Ives Street, London SW3.
All Rights Reserved. International Copyright Secured.

Chorus 1

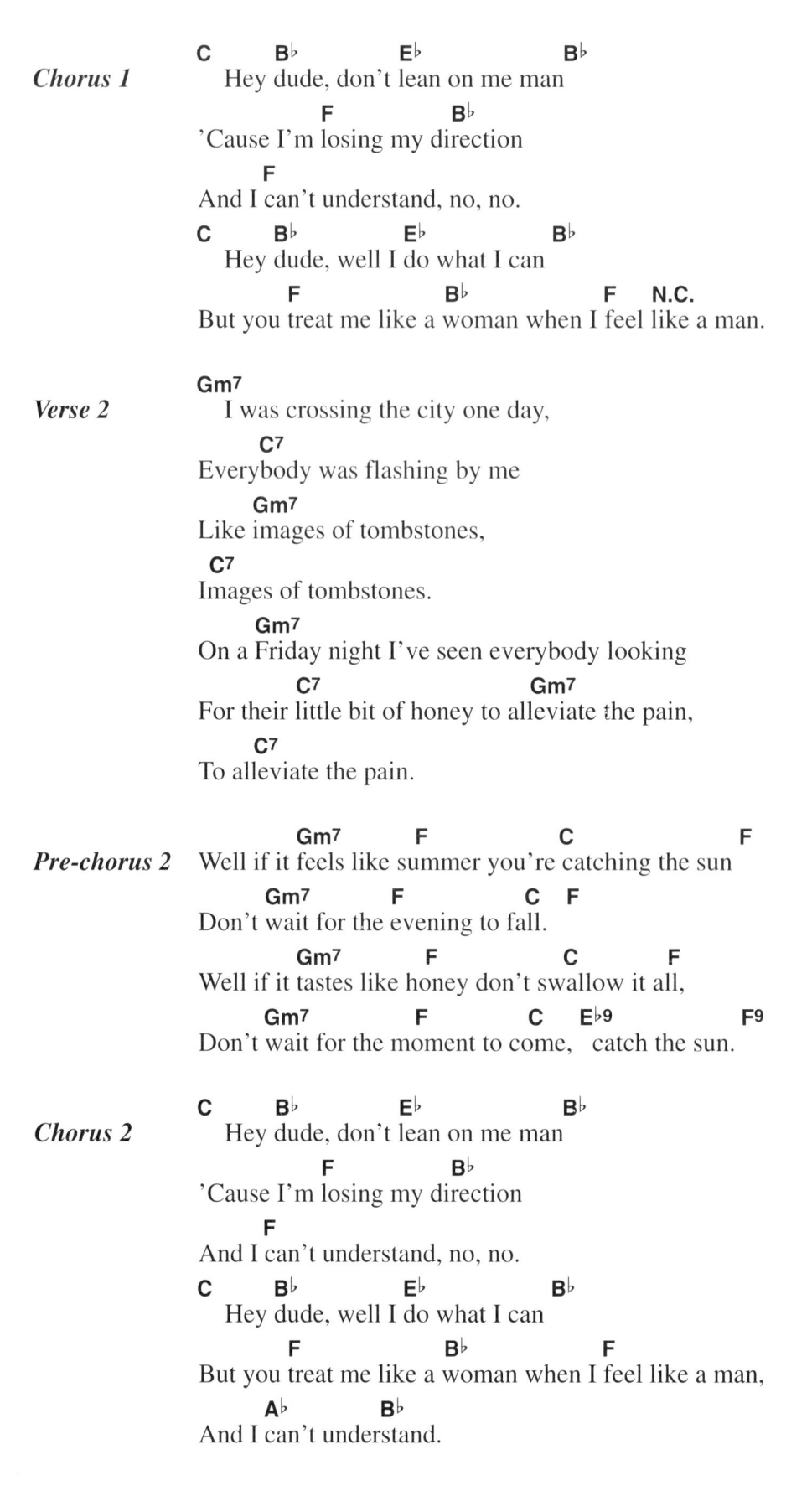

   C B♭   E♭   B♭
    Hey dude, don't lean on me man
      F   B♭
   'Cause I'm losing my direction
     F
   And I can't understand, no, no.
   C B♭   E♭   B♭
    Hey dude, well I do what I can
      F   B♭   F N.C.
   But you treat me like a woman when I feel like a man.

Verse 2

    Gm7
    I was crossing the city one day,
     C7
   Everybody was flashing by me
    Gm7
   Like images of tombstones,
    C7
   Images of tombstones.
    Gm7
   On a Friday night I've seen everybody looking
     C7   Gm7
   For their little bit of honey to alleviate the pain,
    C7
   To alleviate the pain.

Pre-chorus 2

    Gm7 F   C   F
   Well if it feels like summer you're catching the sun
    Gm7 F   C F
   Don't wait for the evening to fall.
    Gm7 F   C   F
   Well if it tastes like honey don't swallow it all,
    Gm7   F C E♭9   F9
   Don't wait for the moment to come, catch the sun.

Chorus 2

   C B♭   E♭   B♭
    Hey dude, don't lean on me man
      F   B♭
   'Cause I'm losing my direction
     F
   And I can't understand, no, no.
   C B♭   E♭   B♭
    Hey dude, well I do what I can
      F   B♭   F
   But you treat me like a woman when I feel like a man,
     A♭ B♭
   And I can't understand.

Middle

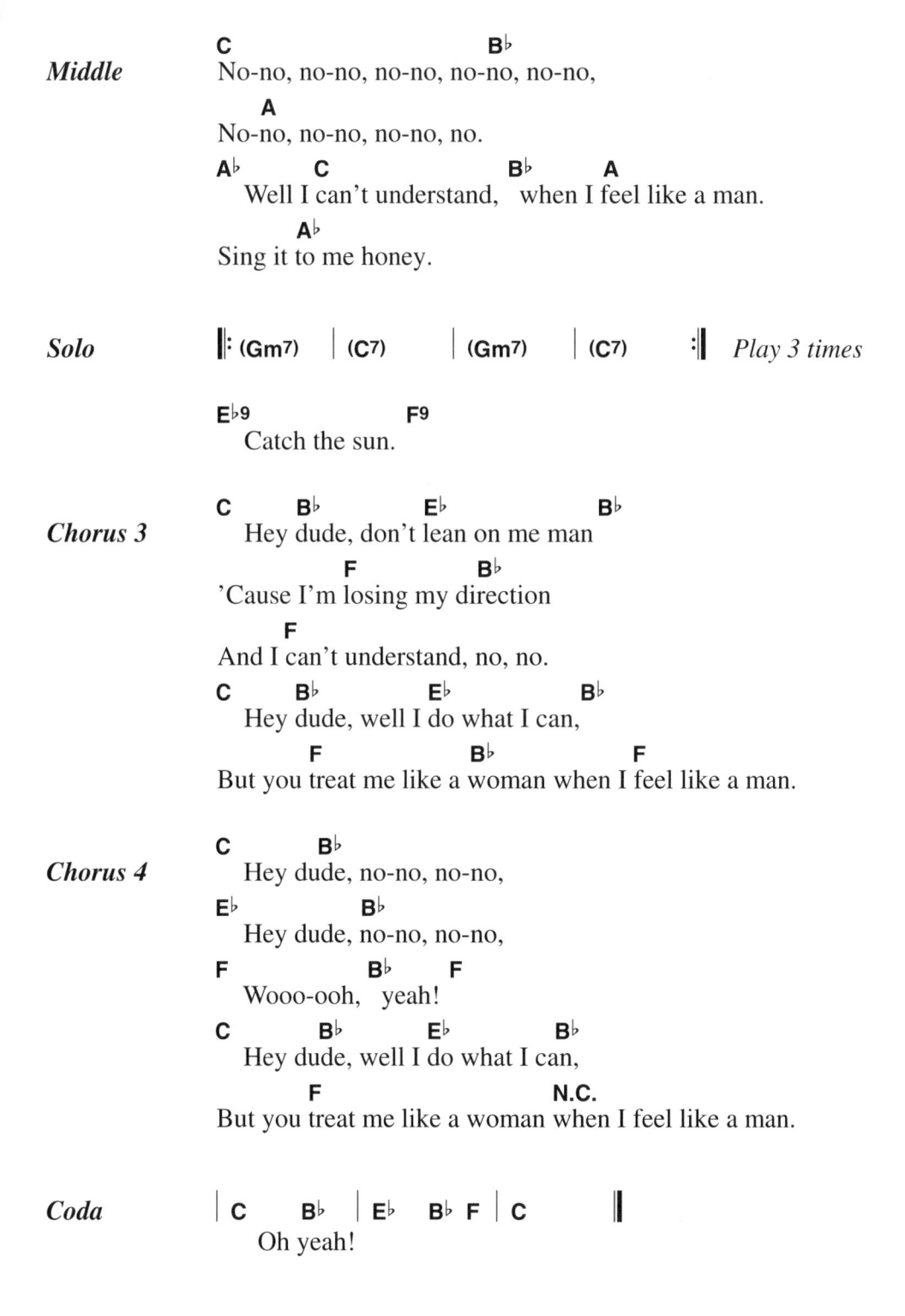

     C   B♭
No-no, no-no, no-no, no-no, no-no,

     A
No-no, no-no, no-no, no.

A♭   C   B♭   A
  Well I can't understand,   when I feel like a man.

         A♭
Sing it to me honey.

Solo

‖: (Gm7) | (C7) | (Gm7) | (C7) :‖ *Play 3 times*

E♭9   F9
  Catch the sun.

Chorus 3

  C   B♭   E♭   B♭
  Hey dude, don't lean on me man

        F   B♭
'Cause I'm losing my direction

      F
And I can't understand, no, no.

  C   B♭   E♭   B♭
  Hey dude, well I do what I can,

       F   B♭   F
But you treat me like a woman when I feel like a man.

Chorus 4

  C   B♭
  Hey dude, no-no, no-no,

E♭   B♭
  Hey dude, no-no, no-no,

F   B♭   F
  Wooo-ooh, yeah!

  C   B♭   E♭   B♭
  Hey dude, well I do what I can,

       F   N.C.
But you treat me like a woman when I feel like a man.

Coda

| C   B♭ | E♭ B♭ F | C   ‖
  Oh yeah!

TATTVA

Words & Music by Crispian Mills, Alonza Bevan, Paul Winter-Hart & Jay Darlington

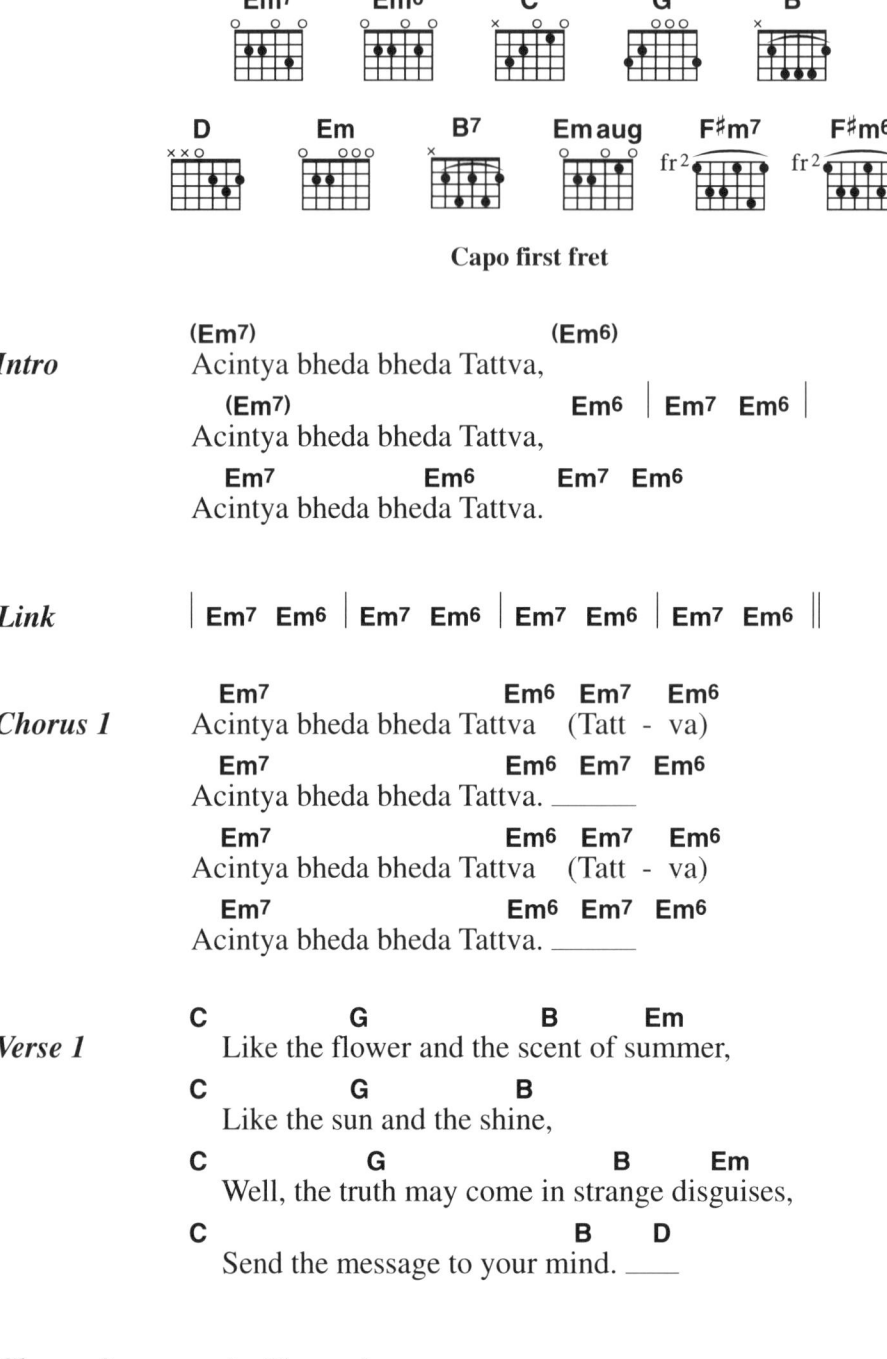

Capo first fret

Intro
        (Em7)   (Em6)
Acintya bheda bheda Tattva,
    (Em7)   Em6 | Em7 Em6 |
Acintya bheda bheda Tattva,
    Em7   Em6   Em7 Em6
Acintya bheda bheda Tattva.

Link
| Em7 Em6 | Em7 Em6 | Em7 Em6 | Em7 Em6 ||

Chorus 1
    Em7   Em6 Em7   Em6
Acintya bheda bheda Tattva (Tatt - va)
    Em7   Em6 Em7   Em6
Acintya bheda bheda Tattva. _____
    Em7   Em6 Em7   Em6
Acintya bheda bheda Tattva (Tatt - va)
    Em7   Em6 Em7   Em6
Acintya bheda bheda Tattva. _____

Verse 1
    C   G   B   Em
Like the flower and the scent of summer,
    C   G   B
Like the sun and the shine,
    C   G   B   Em
Well, the truth may come in strange disguises,
    C   B   D
Send the message to your mind. ___

Chorus 2   As Chorus 1

© Copyright 1995 Hoodoo Music Limited/Hit & Run Music (Publishing) Limited, 30 Ives Street, London SW3.
All Rights Reserved. International Copyright Secured.

Verse 2

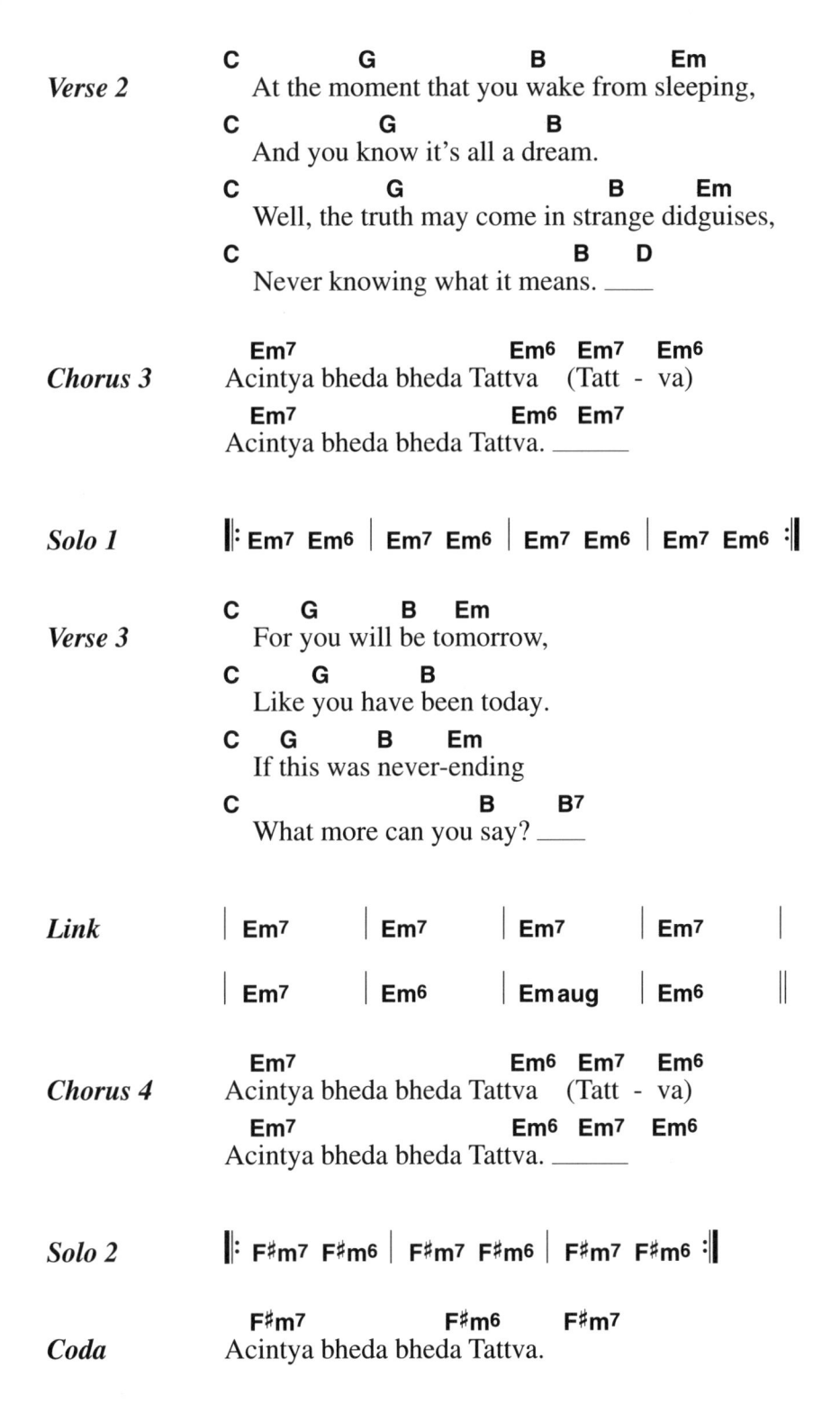

```
      C        G          B       Em
      At the moment that you wake from sleeping,
      C        G          B
      And you know it's all a dream.
      C        G           B        Em
      Well, the truth may come in strange didguises,
      C                    B    D
      Never knowing what it means. ____
```

Chorus 3

```
      Em7              Em6  Em7  Em6
      Acintya bheda bheda Tattva  (Tatt - va)
      Em7              Em6  Em7
      Acintya bheda bheda Tattva. ____
```

Solo 1

```
‖: Em7  Em6 | Em7  Em6 | Em7  Em6 | Em7  Em6 :‖
```

Verse 3

```
      C    G     B   Em
      For you will be tomorrow,
      C    G     B
      Like you have been today.
      C    G     B    Em
      If this was never-ending
      C            B      B7
      What more can you say? ____
```

Link

```
| Em7      | Em7      | Em7      | Em7      |
| Em7      | Em6      | Em aug   | Em6      ‖
```

Chorus 4

```
      Em7              Em6  Em7  Em6
      Acintya bheda bheda Tattva  (Tatt - va)
      Em7              Em6  Em7  Em6
      Acintya bheda bheda Tattva. ____
```

Solo 2

```
‖: F♯m7  F♯m6 | F♯m7  F♯m6 | F♯m7  F♯m6 :‖
```

Coda

```
      F♯m7        F♯m6    F♯m7
      Acintya bheda bheda Tattva.
```

13

BABY CAN I HOLD YOU?

Words & Music by Tracy Chapman

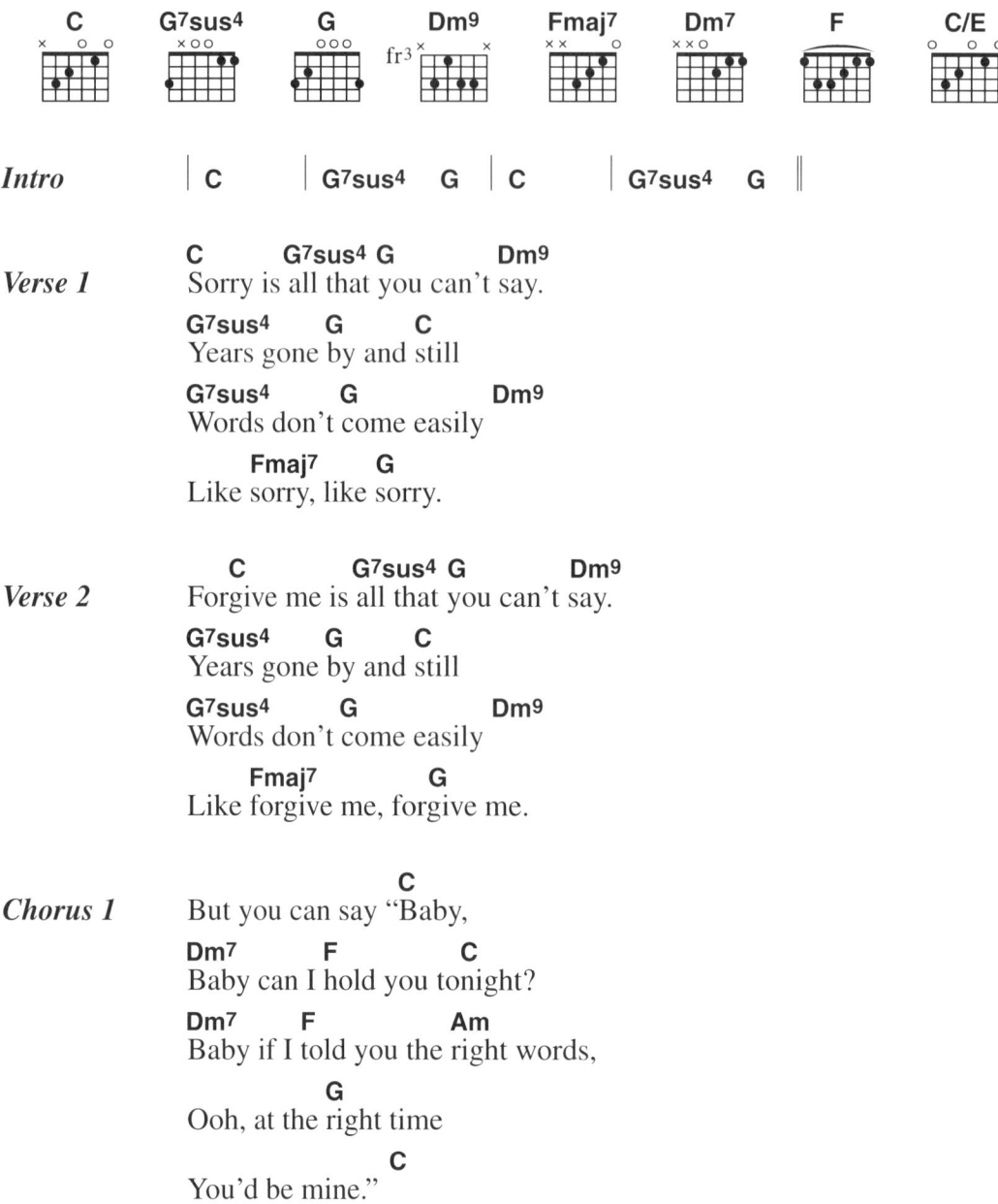

Intro | C | G7sus4 G | C | G7sus4 G ||

Verse 1
      C   G7sus4 G   Dm9
Sorry is all that you can't say.
G7sus4   G   C
Years gone by and still
G7sus4   G   Dm9
Words don't come easily
     Fmaj7   G
Like sorry, like sorry.

Verse 2
       C   G7sus4 G   Dm9
Forgive me is all that you can't say.
G7sus4   G   C
Years gone by and still
G7sus4   G   Dm9
Words don't come easily
     Fmaj7   G
Like forgive me, forgive me.

Chorus 1
              C
But you can say "Baby,
Dm7   F   C
Baby can I hold you tonight?
Dm7   F   Am
Baby if I told you the right words,
         G
Ooh, at the right time
        C
You'd be mine."

© Copyright 1988 Purple Rabbit Music/EMI April Music Incorporated, USA.
EMI Songs Limited, 127 Charing Cross Road, London WC2.
All Rights Reserved. International Copyright Secured.

Link

| Dm   C/E   F   G ||

Verse 3

C   G7sus4 G   Dm9
"I love you" is all that you can't say

G7sus4   G   C
Years gone by and still

G7sus4   G   Dm9
Words don't come easily

          Fmaj7   G
Like "I love you, I love you."

Chorus 2   As Chorus 1

Chorus 3

Dm7   F   C
"Baby can I hold you tonight?

Dm7   F   Am
Baby, if I told you the right words,

             G
Ooh, at the right time

         C
You'd be mine".

Coda

C   Dm7 F
(Baby, if I told you, baby can I hold you?)
                                    C
                                    you'd be mine

C   Dm7 F
(Baby, if I told you, baby can I hold you?)
                                    C
                                    you'd be mine

C   Dm7
(Baby, if I told you)

F   C
Baby, can I hold you?

15

DREAMS

Music by Dolores O'Riordan & Noel Hogan • Words by Dolores O'Riordan

E   Amaj7   B7   E/A   A   G   Csus2

Intro | E | E | Amaj7 | Amaj7 | B7 | B7 | E | E |
| E | E | E/A | E/A | B7 | B7 | E | E ||

Verse 1
        Amaj7
Oh, my life
               B7
Is changing ev'ry day,
              E
In ev'ry possible way.

          Amaj7
And oh, my dreams,
                B7
It's never quite as it seems,
               E
Never quite as it seems.

Verse 2
                        E/A
I know I've felt like this before,
                      B7
But now I'm feeling it even more,
                E
Because it came from you.

                A
And then I open up and see
                 B7
The person falling here is me,
           E
A diff'rent way to be.

Middle
   G   Csus2
Ah, la, la, ah, la, da, ya,
   G   Csus2 E
La, ya, ah, la.

© Copyright 1992 Island Music Limited, 47 British Grove, London W4.
All Rights Reserved. International Copyright Secured.

Verse 3

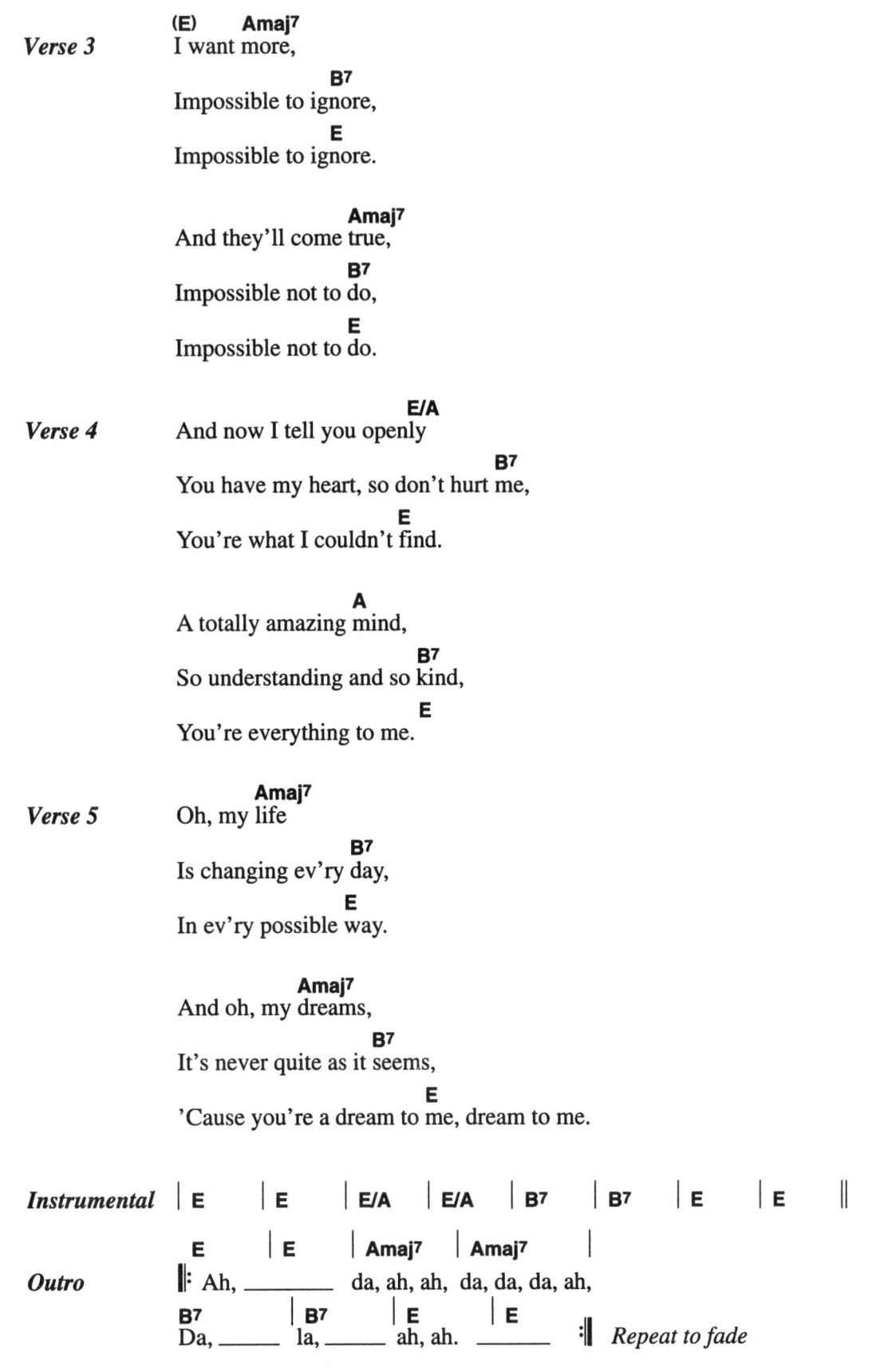

     (E)   **Amaj7**
I want more,
                B7
Impossible to ignore,
           E
Impossible to ignore.

             Amaj7
And they'll come true,
           B7
Impossible not to do,
           E
Impossible not to do.

Verse 4

                E/A
And now I tell you openly
                        B7
You have my heart, so don't hurt me,
                 E
You're what I couldn't find.

             A
A totally amazing mind,
                     B7
So understanding and so kind,
               E
You're everything to me.

Verse 5

        Amaj7
Oh, my life
         B7
Is changing ev'ry day,
        E
In ev'ry possible way.

        Amaj7
And oh, my dreams,
          B7
It's never quite as it seems,
                 E
'Cause you're a dream to me, dream to me.

Instrumental | E | E | E/A | E/A | B7 | B7 | E | E ||

Outro

    E | E | Amaj7 | Amaj7 |
||: Ah, _____ da, ah, ah, da, da, da, ah,
    B7 | B7 | E | E   :||
Da, _____ la, _____ ah, ah. _____   *Repeat to fade*

ENTER SANDMAN

Words & Music by James Hetfield, Lars Ulrich & Kirk Hammett

	E5 A5 G5 F#5 F5 B5

Intro

‖: E5 A5 | E5 A5 | E5 A5 | E5 A5 :‖ *Play 3 times*

‖: E5 | E5 | E5 | E5 :‖ *Play 4 times*

‖: E5 A5 | E5 A5 | E5 A5 | G5 F#5 E5 :‖

Verse 1

E5   F5 E5
 Say your prayers, little one,
E5   F5 E5   G5 F#5 G5 F#5 E5
 Don't forget my son, to include ev'ry one.
E5   F5 E5
 I tuck you in, warm within,
E5   F5 E5   G5   F#5 G5 F#5
 Keep you free from sin 'til the sandman he comes,   ah.

Bridge 1

F#5 B5   F#5 B5
 Sleep with one eye open,
F#5 B5   F#5 B5
 Gripping your pillow tight.

Chorus 1

F#5 B5 F#5 B5 F#5 B5   E5
 Ex - it   light. En - ter night.
F#5 B5 E5   G5   F#5 G5 F#5   E5
 Take my hand. We're off to never-ne - ver land.

Instrumental

‖: (E5) A5 | E5 A5 | E5 A5 | E5 F#5 G5 E5 :‖

Verse 2

E5   F5 E5
 Something's wrong, shut the light,
E5   F5 E5   G5   F#5 G5 F#5 E5
 Heavy thoughts tonight, and they aren't of Snow White.
E5   F5 E5
 Dreams of war dreams of liars,
(E5)   F5 E5   G5   F#5 G5 F#5
 Dreams of dragons fire and of things that will bite,   yeah.

© Copyright 1991 Creeping Death Music, USA.
PolyGram Music Publishing Limited, 47 British Grove, London W4.
All Rights Reserved. International Copyright Secured.

Bridge 2   As Bridge 1

Chorus 2   As Chorus 1

Solo   Over Verse 1, Bridge 1 and Chorus 1 ad lib.

Middle
```
      E5            A5           E5            A5
      Now I lay me down to sleep, (now I lay me down to sleep,)
      E5            A5           E5            A5
      Pray the Lord my soul to keep, (pray the Lord my soul to keep,)
      E5        A5          E5         A5
      If I die before I wake, (if I die before I wake,)
      E5            A5           E5             A5
      Pray the Lord my soul to take, (pray the Lord my soul to take.)
      F#5     B5   F#5      B5
      Hush little baby, don't say a word
      F#5        B5         F#5    B5
        And never mind that noise you heard,
      F#5        B5         F#5    B5
        It's just the beasts under your bed,
      F#5     B5    F#5     B5
        In your closet, in your head.
```

Chorus 3
```
      F#5 B5 F#5   B5 F#5 B5   E5
      Ex - it   light.  En - ter  night.
      F#5           E5
      Grain of sand.
      F#5 B5 F#5   B5 F#5 B5   E5
      Ex - it   light.  En - ter  night.
      F#5  B5   E5          G5    F#5      G5 F#5  E5
      Take  my hand, we're off to never-ne-ver-land,  yeah.
```

Outro

| E5 A5 | E5 A5 | E5 A5 | E5 A5 |

| E5 A5 | E5 A5 | E5 A5 | E5 F#5 G5 E5 |

‖: E5 A5 | E5 A5 | E5 A5 | E5 A5 :‖   *Repeat to fade*

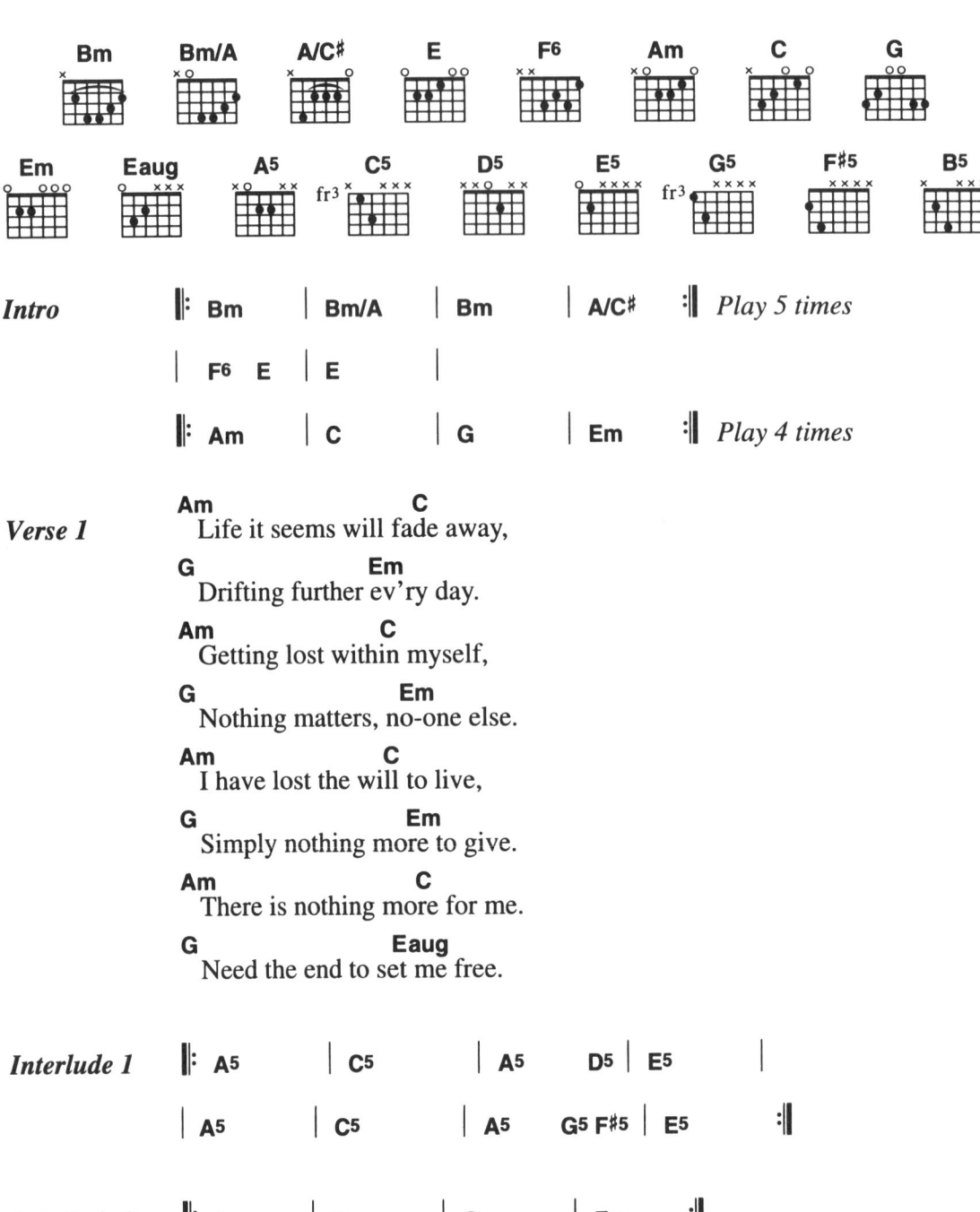

Verse 2

    Am   C
Things not what they used to be,
  G   Em
Missing one inside of me.
  Am   C
Deathly lost, this can't be real,
  G   Em
Cannot stand this hell I feel.
  Am   C
Emptiness is filling me
  G   Em
To the point of agony.
  Am   C
Growing darkness taking dawn,
  G   Eaug
I was me but now he's gone.

Interlude 3   As Interlude 1

Interlude 4   ‖: D5 E5 | D5 E5 G5 F♯5 | D5 | D5 :‖

Bridge 1

D5 E5   D5 E5   G5 F♯5   D5
No one but me can save myself but it's too late.
D5 E5   D5 E5   G5   F♯5 D5
Now I can't think, think why I should even try.

Interlude 5   As Interlude 4

Bridge 2

D5 E5   D5 E5   G5 F♯5   D5
Yesterday seems as though it nev-er existed.
D5 E5   D5 E5   G5 F♯5   D5
Death greets me warm, now I will just say goodbye.

Interlude 6   ‖: E5 | E5 G5 F♯5 | E5 | D5 | D5 :‖

Outro solo   ‖: B5 | B5 | A5 | A5 |
                    | G5 | G5 | A5 | A5 :‖ *Repeat to fade*

FORGIVEN, NOT FORGOTTEN

Words & Music by Andrea Corr, Caroline Corr, Sharon Corr & Jim Corr

Am   C/E   D/F#   C/G   D   Cmaj7   Am/E

Intro

| Am C/E | D/F# | Am C/G | D/F# |

| Am C/E | D/F# | Am C/G | D |

||: Am Cmaj7 | D/F# :||

Verse 1

Am   C/G D/F#   Am/E   C/G   D
All alone,   staring on, watching her life go by
       Am   C/G   D/F#
When her days are grey and her   nights are black,
Am/E   C/G   D
Different shades of mundane.
            Am   C/G
And the one-eyed furry toy
      D/F#
That lies upon the bed
     Am/E C/G   D
Has often heard her cry
             Am   C/G   D/F#
And heard her whisper of a name long forgiven
          Am/E C/G D
But not forgotten.

Chorus

          Am   C/G   D/F#
You're forgiven,   not forgotten
          Am/E C/G   D/F#
You're forgiven,   not forgotten
          Am   C/G   D/F#
You're forgiven,   not forgotten
             Am/E C/G D
You're not forgotten

© Copyright 1995 Beacon Communications Music Corporation/Songs of PolyGram International Incorporated, USA.
PolyGram Music Publishing Limited, 47 British Grove, London W4.
All Rights Reserved. International Copyright Secured.

Verse 2

      Am   **C/G** **D**   **Am/E**   **C/G** **D**
A bleeding heart   torn apart, left on an icy bed
        Am   **C**   **D**
In the room where they once lay   face to face
Am/E   **C**   **D**
Nothing could get in the way
          Am   **C**   **D**
But now the memories of a man are haunting her days
        Am/E **C**   **D**
And the craving never fades
        Am   **C**   **D**   **Am/E** **C/G** **D**
She's still dreaming of a man long forgiven, but not forgotten

Chorus 2   As Chorus 1

Link   ‖: **Am** **C/G** | **D/F♯** :‖ *Play 3 times*

            | **Am/E** **C/G** | **D** ‖

Am **C/G** **D/F♯**   **Am**   **C/G**   **D/F♯**
Still alone,   staring on, wishing her life goodbye
                Am   **C/G**
As she goes searching for the man
        D/F♯   **Am** **C/G** **D/F♯**
Long forgiven, but not forgotten

Chorus 3   **Am** **C**   **D**
         ‖: You're forgiven, not forgotten. :‖ *Play 8 times*

Coda   **N.C**
You're not forgotten, you're not forgotten

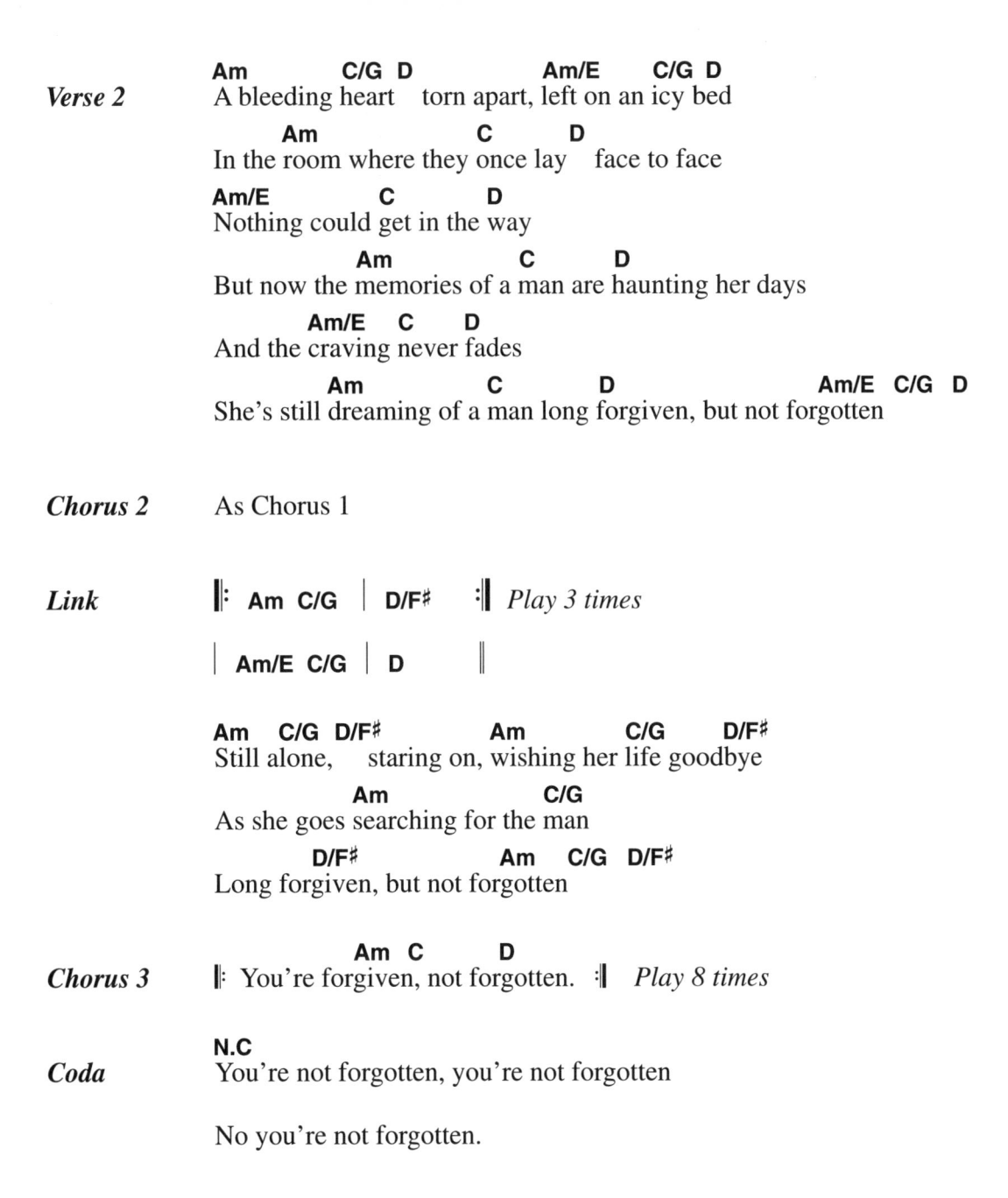

No you're not forgotten.

WHAT CAN I DO

Words & Music by Andrea Corr, Caroline Corr, Sharon Corr & Jim Corr

A   E/G#   D   A/C#   E   Bm7   F#m   Dmaj7

Intro
    A   E/G#
Do do do do   do do do do
    D
Do do do   do do do,
    A/C#   E
Do do do do   do do do do
    Bm7
Do do do   do do do.

Verse 1
    A   E/G#   D
I haven't slept at all in days
    A/C#   E   Bm7
It's been so long since we've talked
    A   E/G#   D
And I have been here many ti___ mes
    A/C#   E   Bm7
I just don't know what I'm doing wrong.

Chorus 1
    A   E/G#   D
What can I do to make you love me?
    A/C#   E   Bm7
What can I do to make you care?
    A   E/G#   D
What can I say to make you feel this?
    A/C#   E   Bm7
What can I do to get you there?

© Copyright 1997 Beacon Communications Music Corporation/Songs of PolyGram International Incorporated, USA.
PolyGram Music Publishing Limited, 47 British Grove, London W4.
All Rights Reserved. International Copyright Secured.

Verse 2

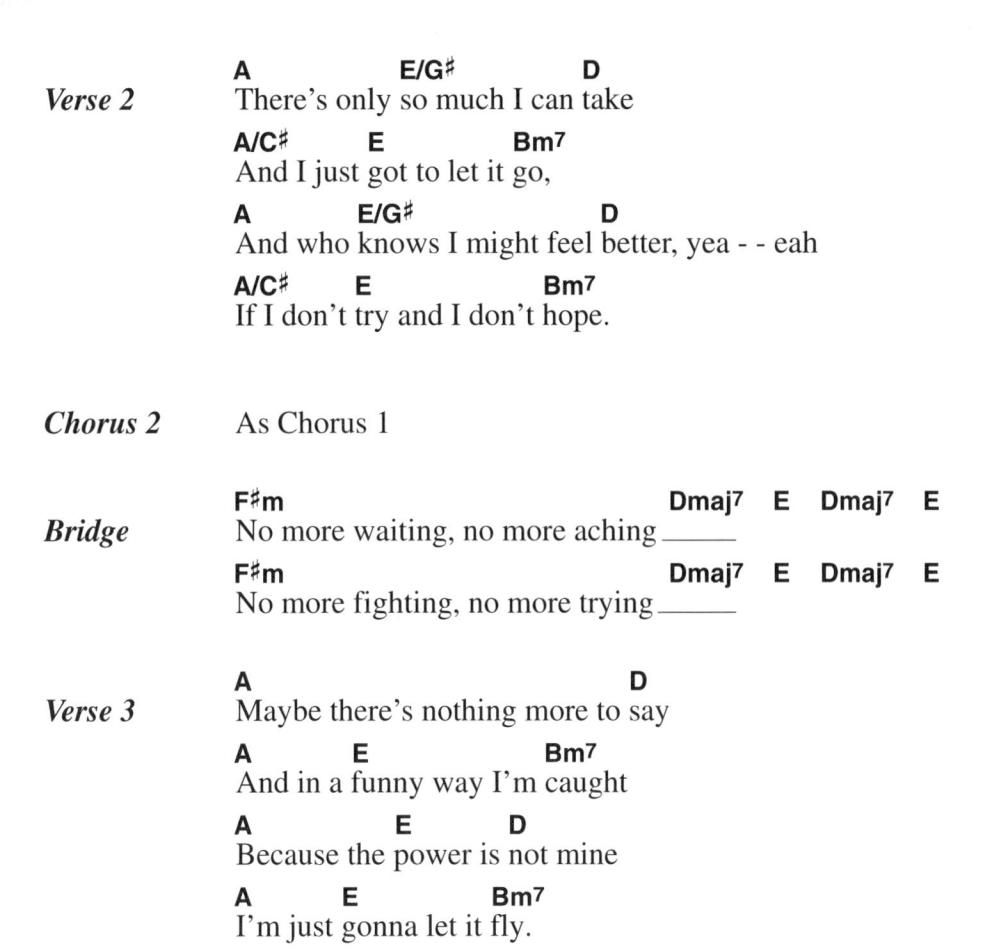

      A   E/G♯   D
There's only so much I can take

  A/C♯   E   Bm7
And I just got to let it go,

    A   E/G♯   D
And who knows I might feel better, yea - - eah

  A/C♯   E   Bm7
If I don't try and I don't hope.

Chorus 2   As Chorus 1

Bridge

  F♯m   Dmaj7 E Dmaj7 E
No more waiting, no more aching ____

  F♯m   Dmaj7 E Dmaj7 E
No more fighting, no more trying ____

Verse 3

  A   D
Maybe there's nothing more to say

  A   E   Bm7
And in a funny way I'm caught

  A   E   D
Because the power is not mine

  A   E   Bm7
I'm just gonna let it fly.

Chorus 3

     A   E   D
What can I do to make you love me?
     A   E   Bm7
What can I do to make you care?
     A   E   D
What can I say to make you feel this?
     A   E   Bm7
What can I do to get you there?

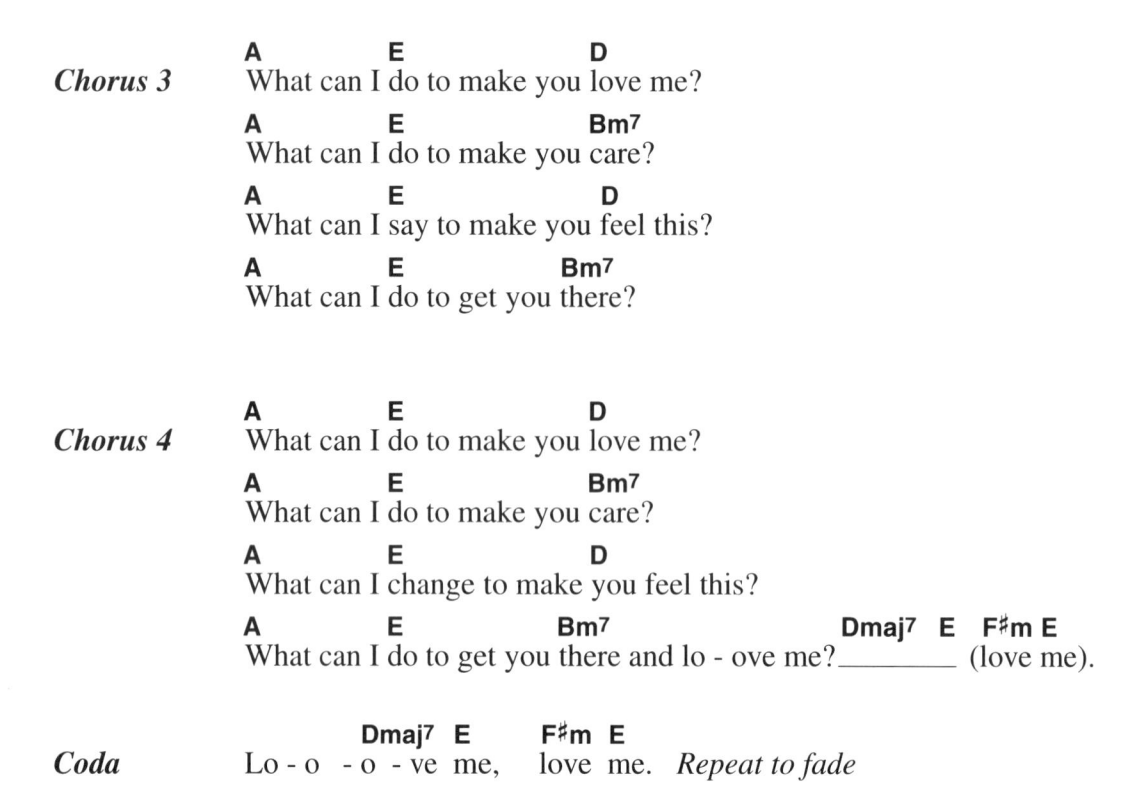

Chorus 4

     A   E   D
What can I do to make you love me?
     A   E   Bm7
What can I do to make you care?
     A   E   D
What can I change to make you feel this?
     A   E   Bm7   Dmaj7 E F♯m E
What can I do to get you there and lo - ove me?_____ (love me).

Coda

              Dmaj7 E   F♯m E
Lo - o - o - ve me,   love me. *Repeat to fade*

THAT'S ENTERTAINMENT

Words & Music by Paul Weller

G   Em7   Em   Am7   Fmaj7

Capo third fret

Intro
| G | Em7 Em | G | Em7 Em |
| Am7 | Fmaj7 | G | Em7 Em ||

Verse 1
G   Em7   Em
A police car and a screaming siren,
G   Em7   Em
Pneumatic drill and ripped up concrete.
G   Em7   Em
A baby wailing, stray dog howling,
G   Em7   Em
A screech of brakes, a lamp light blinking.
Am7   Fmaj7
That's entertainment,
Am7   Fmaj7 | G | Em7 Em ||
That's entertainment.

Verse 2
G   Em7   Em
A smash of glass and the rumble of _ boots,
G   Em7   Em
An electric train and a _ ripped up _ phone booth.
G   Em7   Em
Paint splattered walls and the cry of a tom cat,
G   Em7   Em
Lights going out and a _ kick in the balls, I say:
Am7   Fmaj7
That's entertainment,
Am   Fmaj7
That's entertainment.
G   Em7   Em
Ah, la la la la la,
G   Em7   Em
Ah, la la la la la.

© Copyright 1980 Stylist Music Limited/
BMG Music Publishing Limited, Bedford House, 69-79 Fulham High Street, London SW6.
This arrangement © Copyright 1999 BMG Music Publishing Limited.
All Rights Reserved. International Copyright Secured.

Verse 3

    G   Em7 Em
    Days of speed and slow time Mondays,
    G   Em7 Em
    Pissing down with rain on a boring Wednesday.
    G   Em7 Em
    Watching the news and not eating your tea,
    G   Em7   Em
    A freezing cold flat and damp on the walls, I say:

Am7   **Fmaj7**
That's entertainment,

Am7   **Fmaj7** | G | Em7 Em |
That's entertainment.

    G | Em7   Em
      La la la la la,
    G | Em7   Em
      La la la la la.

Verse 4

    G   Em7   Em
    Waking up at six a.m. on a cool warm morning,
    G   Em7 Em
    Opening the windows and breathing in petrol.
    G   Em7 Em
    An amateur band rehearsing in a nearby yard,
    G   Em7   Em
    Watching the telly and thinking about your holidays.

Am7   **Fmaj7**
That's entertainment,

Am7   **Fmaj7**
That's entertainment.

G Em7 Em
Ah, la la la la la,

G Em7 Em
Ah, la la la la la,

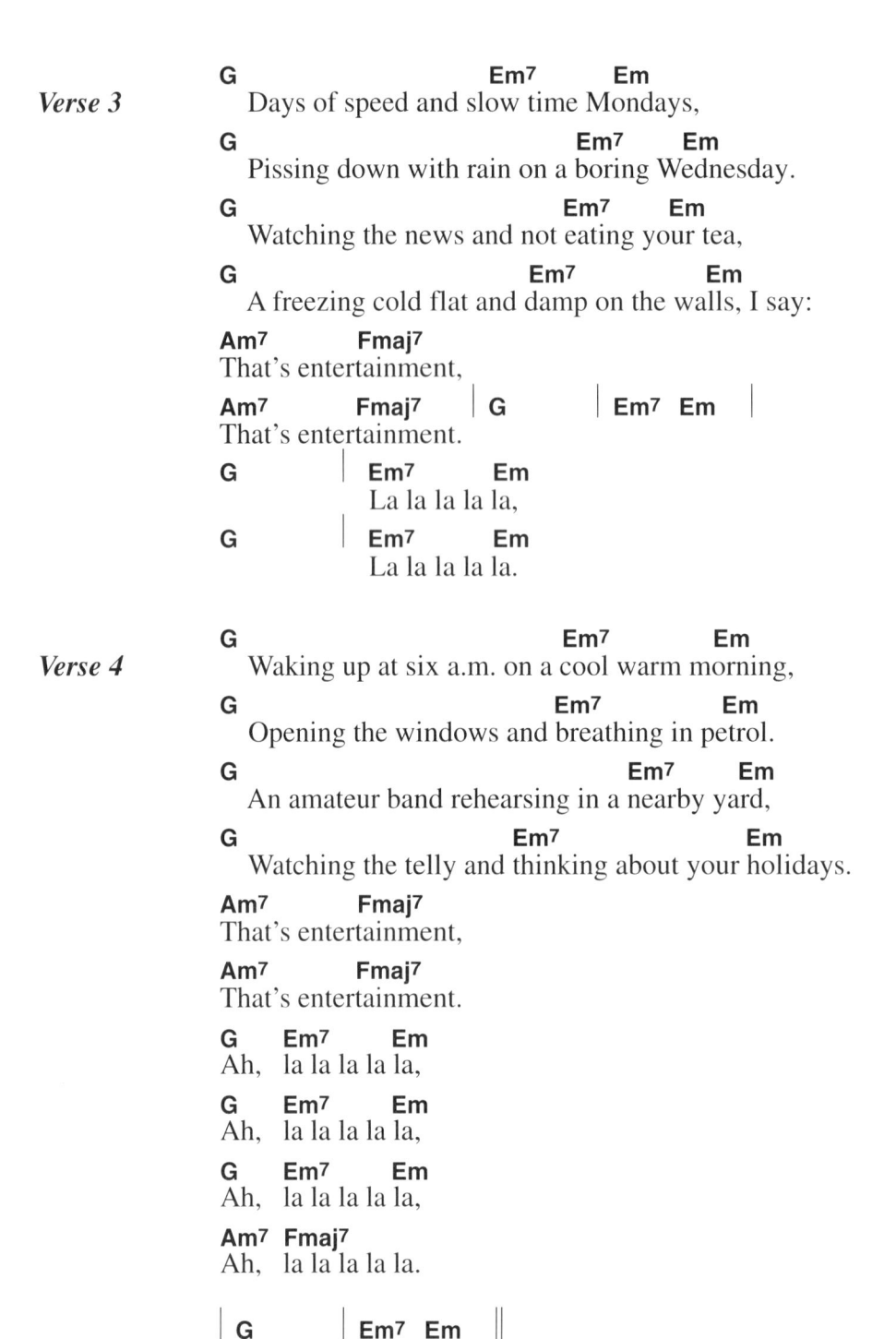

G Em7 Em
Ah, la la la la la,

Am7 **Fmaj7**
Ah, la la la la la.

    | G | Em7 Em ||

Verse 5

      G   Em7   Em
Waking up from bad dreams and smoking cigarettes.

      G   Em7   Em
Cuddling a warm girl and smelling stale perfume.

      G   Em7   Em
A hot summer's day and sticky black tarmac,

      G   Em7   Em
Feeding ducks in the park and wishing you were far away.

Am7   **Fmaj7**
That's entertainment,

Am7   **Fmaj7** | G | Em7 Em ||
That's entertainment.

Verse 6

      G   Em7   Em
Two lovers kissing amongst the screams of midnight,

      G   Em7   Em
Two lovers missing the tranquility of solitude.

      G   Em7   Em
Getting a cab and travelling on buses,

      G   Em7   Em
Reading the graffiti about slashed seat affairs, I say:

Am7   **Fmaj7**
That's entertainment,

Am7   **Fmaj7**
That's entertainment.

||: **G**   **Em7**   **Em**
   Ah, la la la la la,

G   **Em7**   **Em**
Ah, la la la la la,

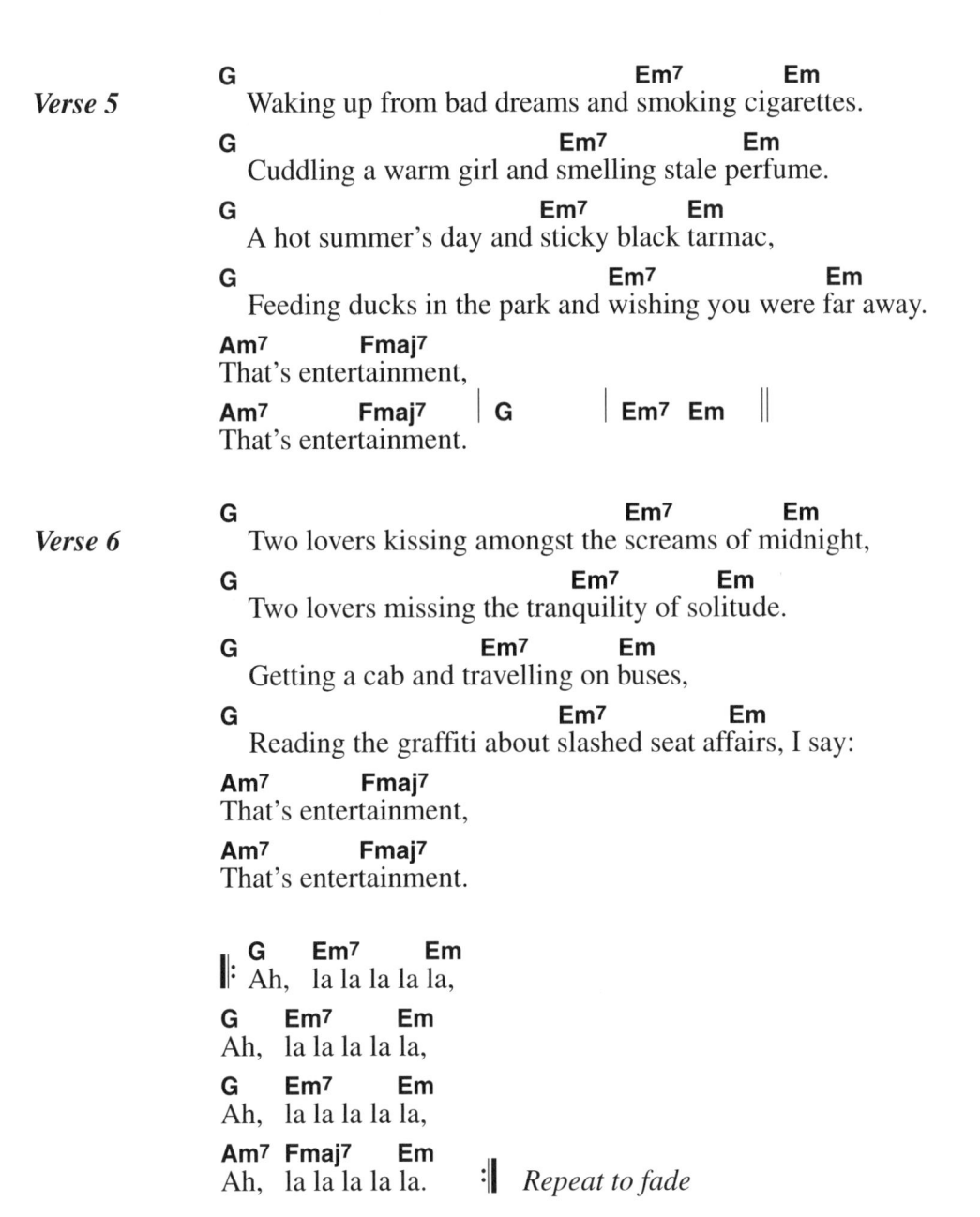

G   **Em7**   **Em**
Ah, la la la la la,

Am7 Fmaj7 **Em**
Ah, la la la la la. :|| *Repeat to fade*

THE BITTEREST PILL (I EVER HAD TO SWALLOW)

Words & Music by Paul Weller

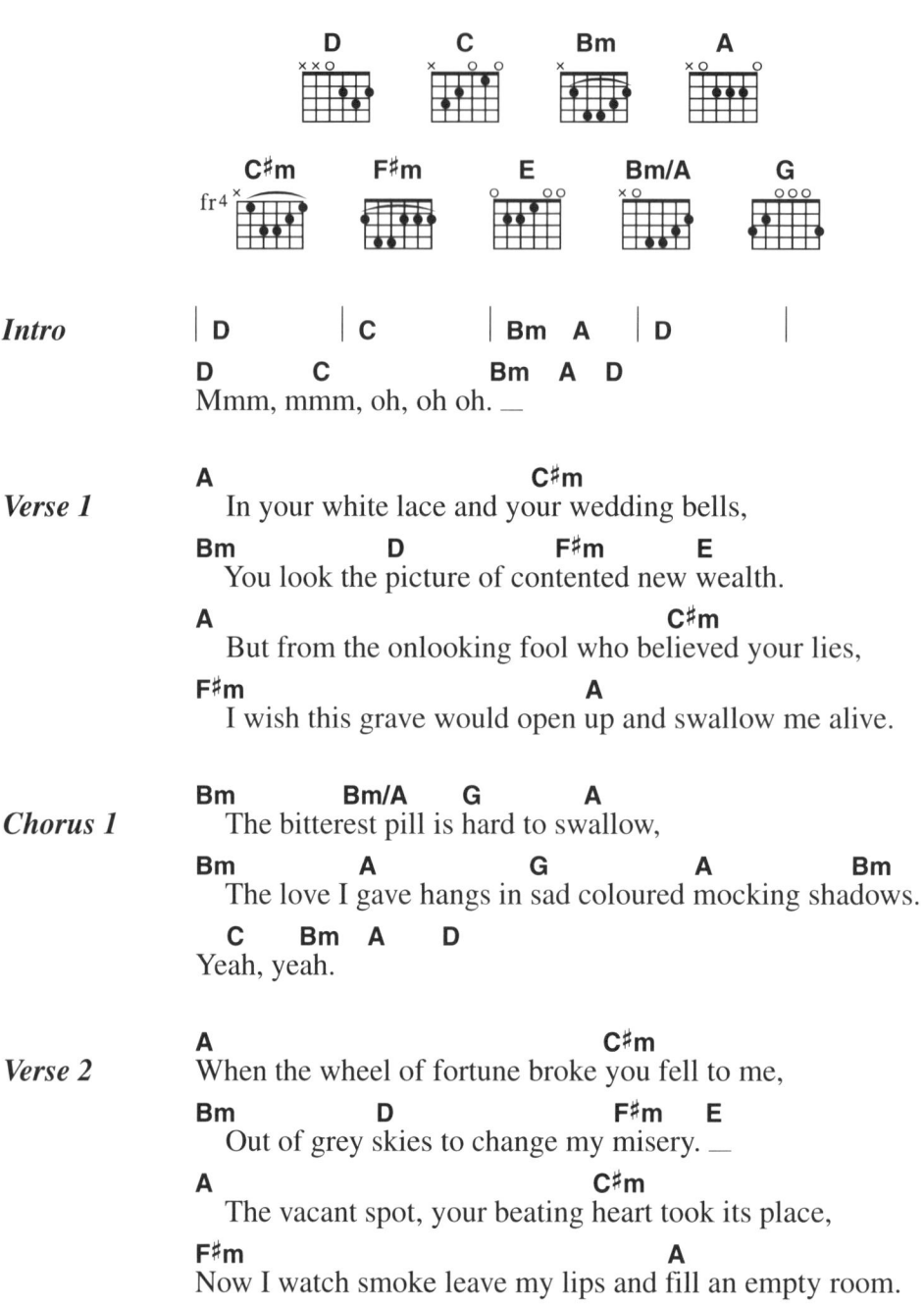

Intro | D | C | Bm A | D |

D   C   Bm   A   D
Mmm, mmm, oh, oh oh. __

Verse 1

A   C#m
   In your white lace and your wedding bells,
Bm   D   F#m   E
   You look the picture of contented new wealth.
A   C#m
   But from the onlooking fool who believed your lies,
F#m   A
   I wish this grave would open up and swallow me alive.

Chorus 1

Bm   Bm/A   G   A
   The bitterest pill is hard to swallow,
Bm   A   G   A   Bm
   The love I gave hangs in sad coloured mocking shadows.
    C   Bm   A   D
Yeah, yeah.

Verse 2

A   C#m
When the wheel of fortune broke you fell to me,
Bm   D   F#m   E
   Out of grey skies to change my misery. __
A   C#m
   The vacant spot, your beating heart took its place,
F#m   A
   Now I watch smoke leave my lips and fill an empty room.

© Copyright 1982 Notting Hill Music (UK) Limited, 8B Berkeley Gardens, London W8.
All Rights Reserved. International Copyright Secured.

Chorus 2

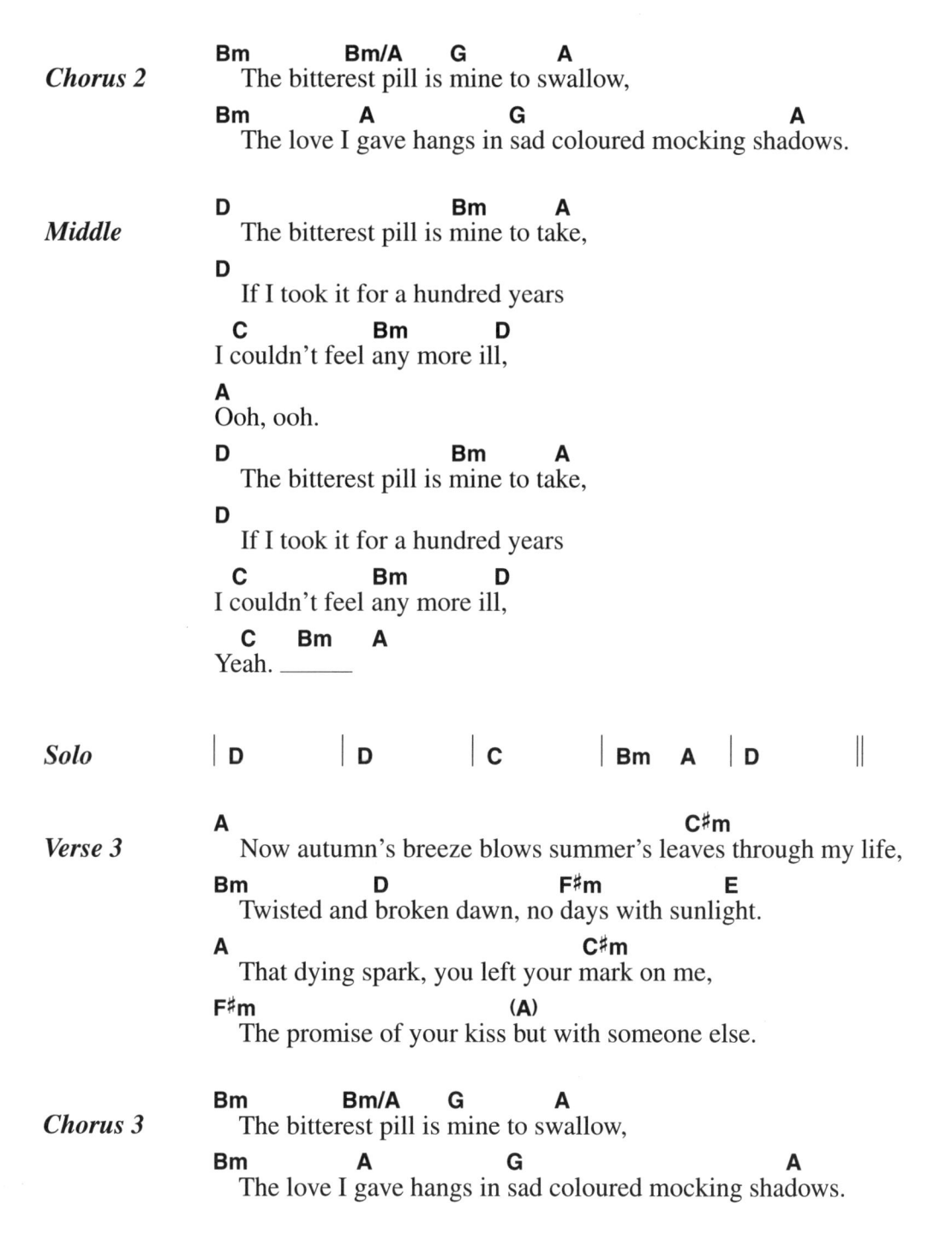

     Bm   Bm/A   G   A
The bitterest pill is mine to swallow,
     Bm   A   G   A
The love I gave hangs in sad coloured mocking shadows.

Middle

    D   Bm   A
The bitterest pill is mine to take,
    D
If I took it for a hundred years
     C   Bm   D
I couldn't feel any more ill,
    A
Ooh, ooh.
    D   Bm   A
The bitterest pill is mine to take,
    D
If I took it for a hundred years
     C   Bm   D
I couldn't feel any more ill,
     C   Bm   A
Yeah. _____

Solo

| D | D | C | Bm   A | D ||

Verse 3

    A   C♯m
Now autumn's breeze blows summer's leaves through my life,
Bm   D   F♯m   E
Twisted and broken dawn, no days with sunlight.
    A   C♯m
That dying spark, you left your mark on me,
F♯m   (A)
The promise of your kiss but with someone else.

Chorus 3

     Bm   Bm/A   G   A
The bitterest pill is mine to swallow,
     Bm   A   G   A
The love I gave hangs in sad coloured mocking shadows.

31

Outro

     D   Bm   A
The bitterest pill is mine to take,
D
If I took it for a hundred years
 C   Bm   D A
I couldn't feel any more ill.
D   Bm   A
The bitterest pill is mine to take,
D
If I took it for a hundred years
 C   Bm   A
I couldn't feel any more ill,

Yeah, ah, ah.

D   Bm   A
The bitterest pill is mine to take,
D
If I took it for a hundred years
 C   Bm   D
I couldn't feel any more ill,
A
Ooh, ooh.
D   Bm   A
The bitterest pill is mine to take,
D
If I took it for a hundred years
 C   Bm   A
I couldn't feel any more ill, ill,

Yeah, yeah.

|: D | Bm | D | C Bm :| *Repeat to fade*

THE ETON RIFLES

Words & Music by Paul Weller

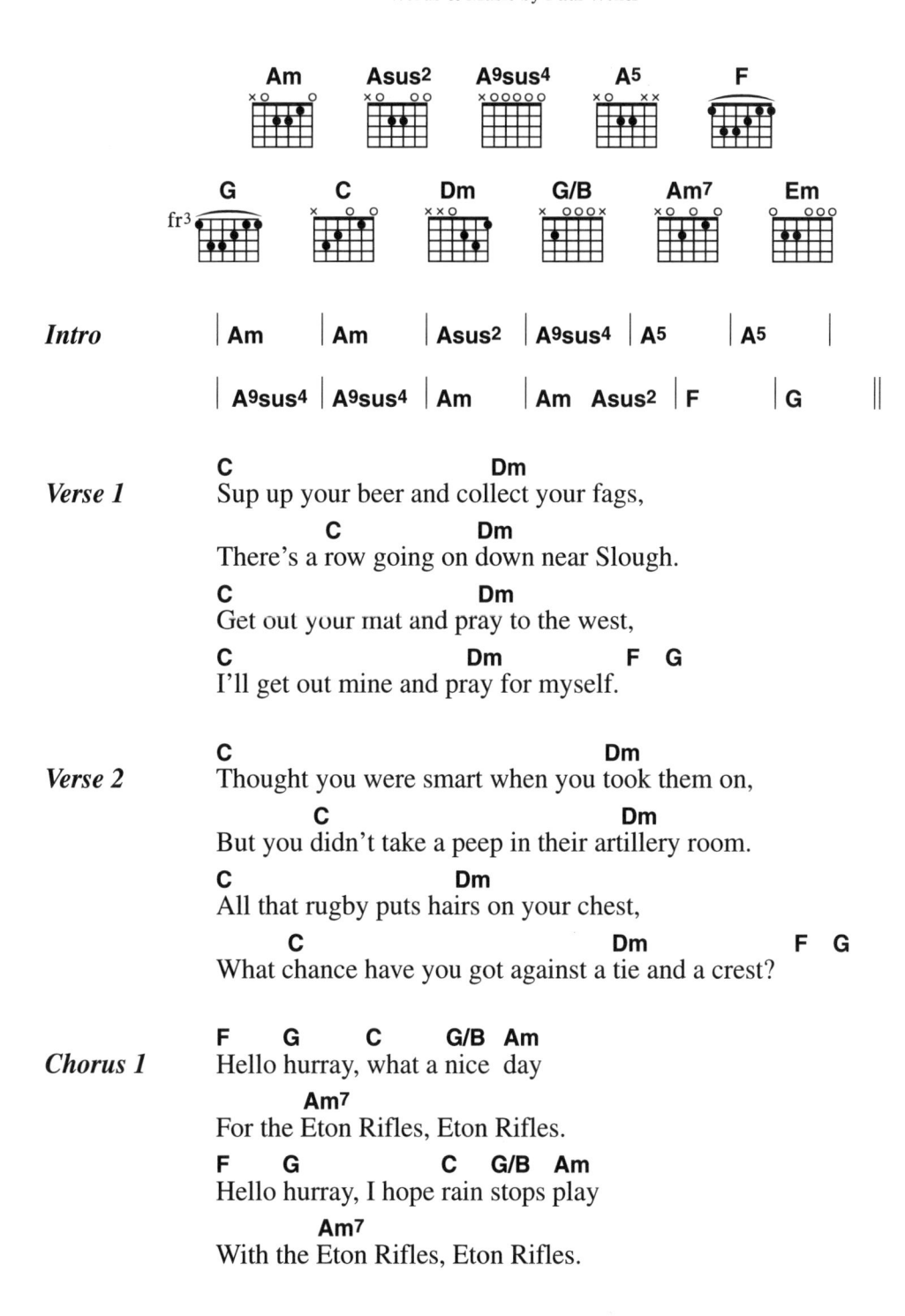

Am Asus2 A9sus4 A5 F

G C Dm G/B Am7 Em

Intro
| Am | Am | Asus2 | A9sus4 | A5 | A5 |
| A9sus4 | A9sus4 | Am | Am Asus2 | F | G ||

Verse 1
C   Dm
Sup up your beer and collect your fags,
    C   Dm
There's a row going on down near Slough.
C   Dm
Get out your mat and pray to the west,
C   Dm   F G
I'll get out mine and pray for myself.

Verse 2
C   Dm
Thought you were smart when you took them on,
       C   Dm
But you didn't take a peep in their artillery room.
C   Dm
All that rugby puts hairs on your chest,
            C   Dm   F G
What chance have you got against a tie and a crest?

Chorus 1
F   G   C   G/B Am
Hello hurray, what a nice day
            Am7
For the Eton Rifles, Eton Rifles.
F   G   C   G/B Am
Hello hurray, I hope rain stops play
            Am7
With the Eton Rifles, Eton Rifles.

© Copyright 1979 Stylist Music Limited/
BMG Music Publishing Limited, Bedford House, 69-79 Fulham High Street, London SW6.
This arrangement © Copyright 1999 BMG Music Publishing Limited.
All Rights Reserved. International Copyright Secured.

Verse 3

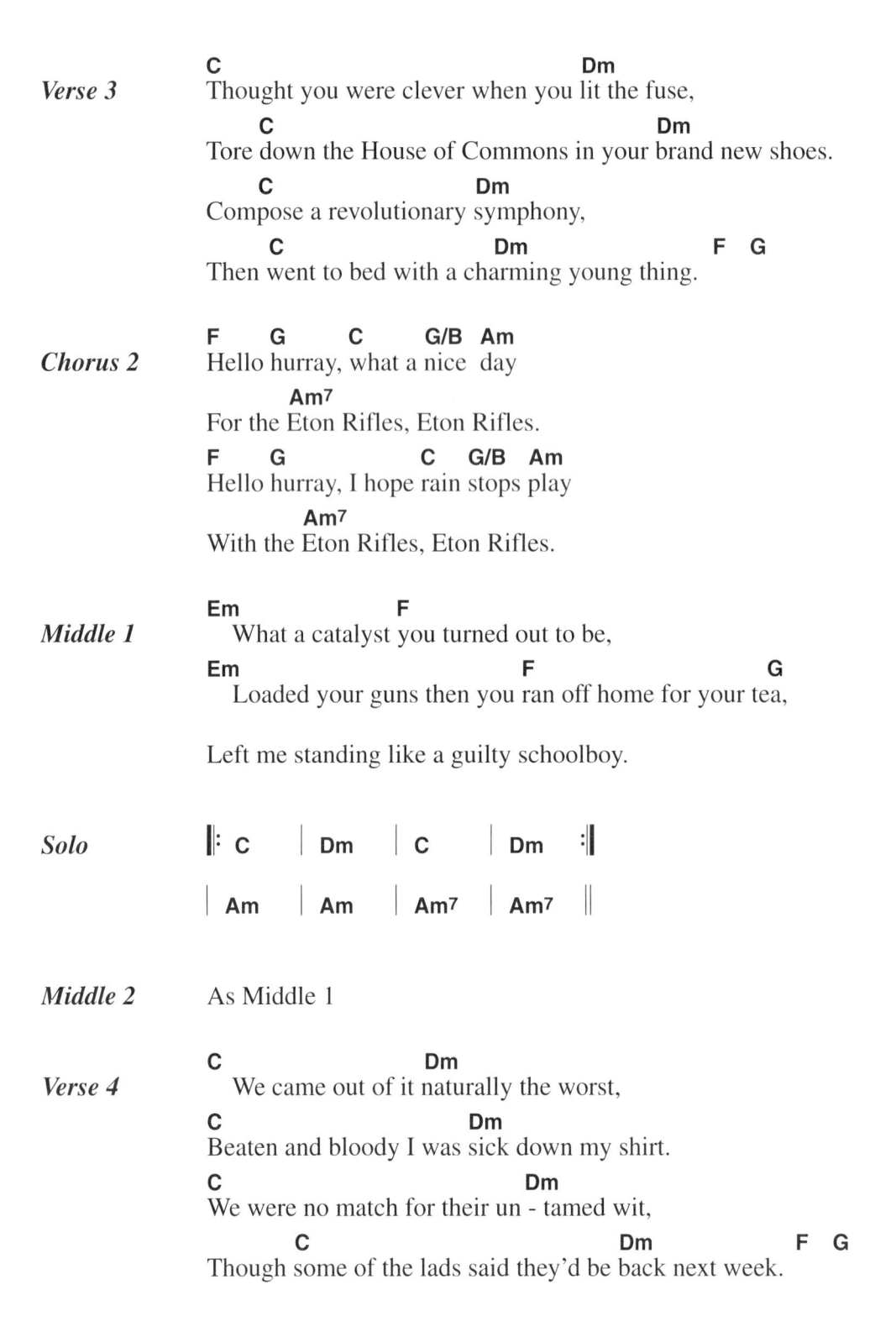

      C   Dm
Thought you were clever when you lit the fuse,
                C   Dm
Tore down the House of Commons in your brand new shoes.
              C   Dm
Compose a revolutionary symphony,
                C   Dm   F G
Then went to bed with a charming young thing.

Chorus 2

       F   G   C   G/B Am
Hello hurray, what a nice day
             Am7
For the Eton Rifles, Eton Rifles.
     F   G   C   G/B Am
Hello hurray, I hope rain stops play
          Am7
With the Eton Rifles, Eton Rifles.

Middle 1

Em   F
   What a catalyst you turned out to be,
Em   F   G
   Loaded your guns then you ran off home for your tea,

Left me standing like a guilty schoolboy.

Solo

|: C | Dm | C | Dm   :|

| Am | Am | Am7 | Am7 ||

Middle 2   As Middle 1

Verse 4

   C   Dm
  We came out of it naturally the worst,
C   Dm
Beaten and bloody I was sick down my shirt.
C   Dm
We were no match for their un - tamed wit,
          C   Dm   F G
Though some of the lads said they'd be back next week.

Chorus 3

    F   G   C   G/B Am
Hello hurray, there's a price to   pay
          Am7
To the Eton Rifles, Eton Rifles.
  F   G   C G/B Am
Hello hurray, I'd prefer the   plague
          Am7
To the Eton Rifles, Eton Rifles.

Chorus 4

    F   G   C   G/B Am
Hello hurray, there's a price to   pay
          Am7
To the Eton rifles, Eton Rifles.
  F   G   C G/B Am
Hello hurray, I'd prefer the   plague
          Am7
To the Eton rifles, Eton Rifles.

Eton rifles, Eton Rifles.

Outro

| A5 | A5 | Asus2 | Asus2 |

| Am | Am | Asus2 | Asus2 |

| A5 | Asus2 | Asus2 | Asus2 | Am7 | Am7 |

                         Asus2
Eton Rifles, Eton Rifles.

LOVE SPREADS

Words & Music by John Squire

Chords: D7 Dm7 (fr5) G D A F C

Intro

‖: D7 | D7 | D7 | D7 :‖

‖: Dm7 | Dm7 | Dm7 | Dm7 :‖

‖: G | G | D | D :‖

| A | A | D | D ‖

Verse 1

Dm7
Love spreads her arms, waits there for the nails;

"I forgive you, boy, I will prevail."

Too much to take, some cross to bear,

I'm hiding in the trees with a picnic, she's over there, yeah.
       Dm7 **G**
Yeah, yeah, yeah,
       Dm7 | A | A | D | D ‖
Yeah, yeah, yeah.

Verse 2

Dm7
She didn't scream, she didn't make a sound.

"I forgive you boy, but don't leave town."

Cold black skin, naked in the rain,

Hammer flash in the lightning, they're hurting her again.
A | A | D |
Oh. ___

© Copyright 1994 Sony/ATV Music Publishing (UK) Limited, 10 Great Marlborough Street, London W1.
All Rights Reserved. International Copyright Secured.

Chorus 1

      D
Let me put you in the picture,
      F
Let me show you what I mean:
      G
The Messiah is my sister
      D
Ain't no king, man, she's my queen.
      D
Let me put you in the picture,
      F
Let me show you what I mean:
      G
The Messiah is my sister
      D
Ain't no king, man, she's my queen.
      C   **A**
I had a dream, I've seen the light
      G   **F**
Don't put it out, 'cause she's alright, yeah, she's my sister.

Link | D | D | D | D ||

Verse 3

Dm7
She didn't scream, she didn't make a sound.

"I forgive you boy, but don't leave town."

Cold black skin, naked in the rain,

Hammer flash in the lightning, they're hurting her again.
G   **Dm7** | **Dm7** | **G** |
Oh, ___ oh, oh, oh.
          Dm7 | **Dm7** | **A** | **A** | **D** | **D** | **D** | **D** | **D** ||
Yeah, yeah, yeah.

Chorus 2

      D
||: Let me put you in the picture,
      F
Let me show you what I mean:
      G
The Messiah is my sister
      D
Ain't no king, man, she's my queen. :|| *Play 8 times*
      C   **A**
I had a dream, I've seen the light
      G   **F**   **D**
Don't put it out, 'cause she's alright, yeah, she's my sister.

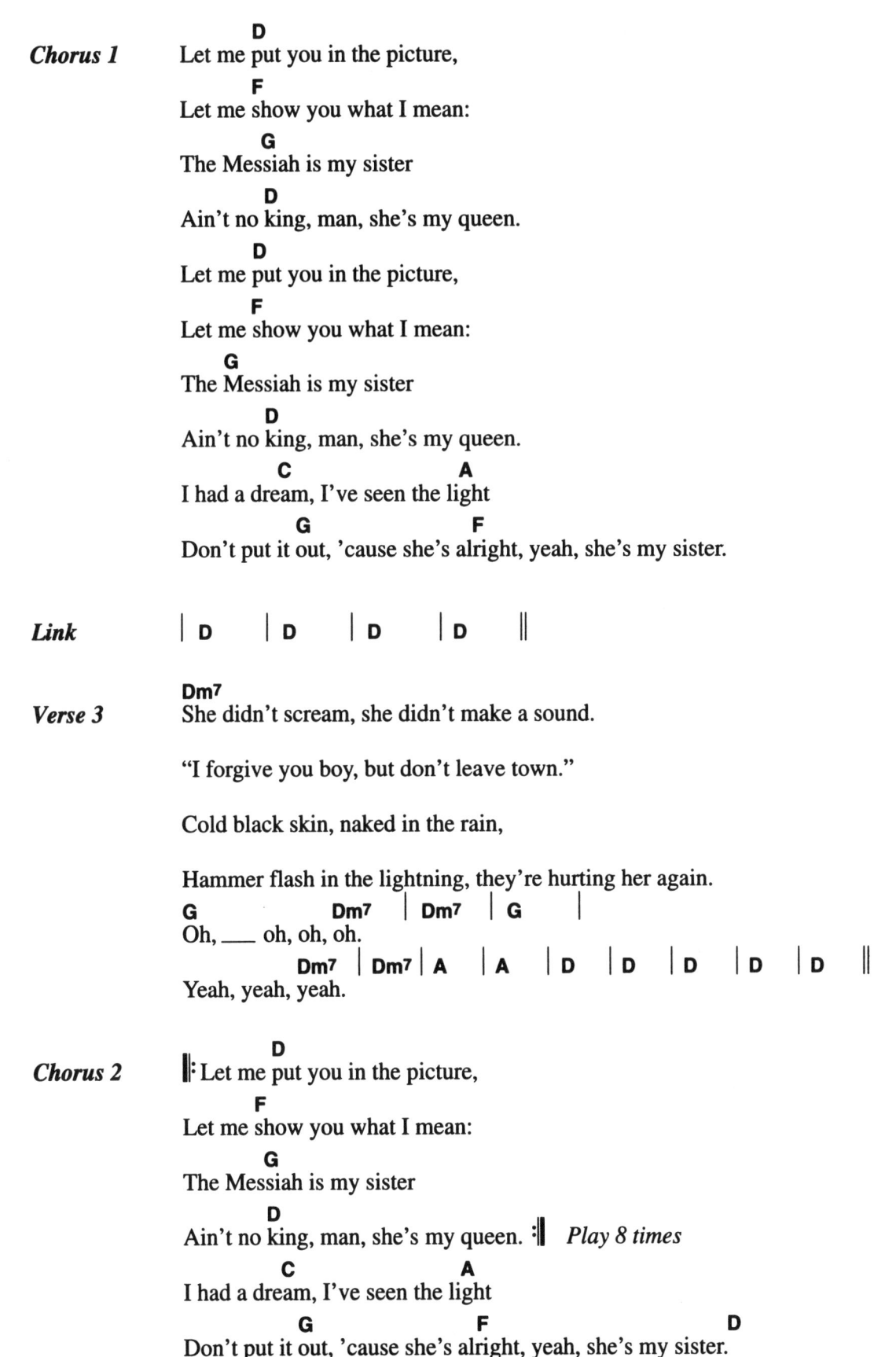

SUNFLOWER

Words & Music by Paul Weller

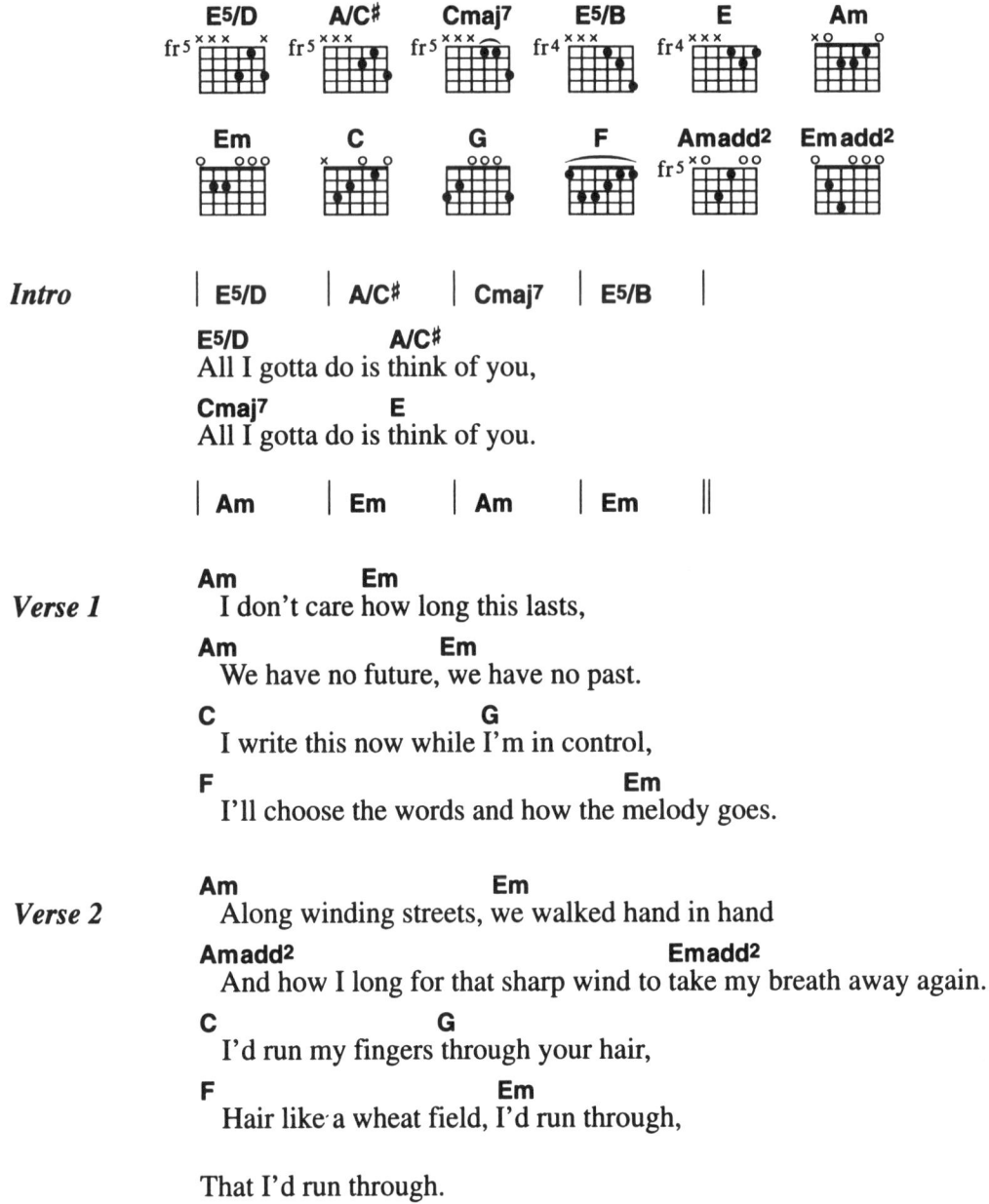

Intro | E5/D | A/C# | Cmaj7 | E5/B |

E5/D   **A/C#**
All I gotta do is think of you,
Cmaj7   **E**
All I gotta do is think of you.

| Am | Em | Am | Em ||

Verse 1
Am   **Em**
I don't care how long this lasts,
Am   **Em**
We have no future, we have no past.
C   **G**
I write this now while I'm in control,
F   **Em**
I'll choose the words and how the melody goes.

Verse 2
Am   **Em**
Along winding streets, we walked hand in hand
Amadd2   **Emadd2**
And how I long for that sharp wind to take my breath away again.
C   **G**
I'd run my fingers through your hair,
F   **Em**
Hair like a wheat field, I'd run through,

That I'd run through.

© Copyright 1993 Notting Hill Music (UK) Limited, 8B Berkeley Gardens, London W8 4AP.
All Rights Reserved. International Copyright Secured.

Chorus 1

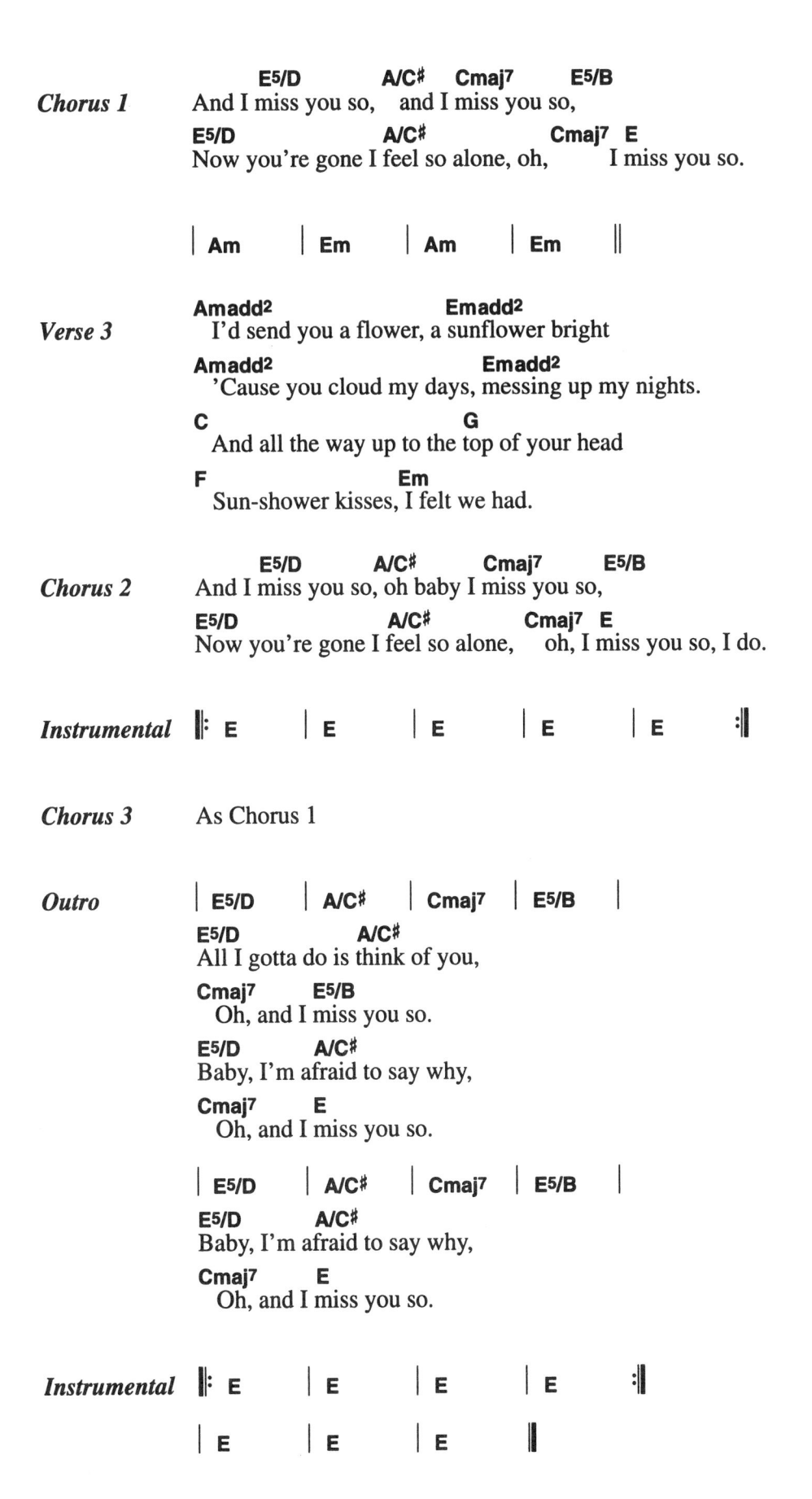

       E5/D   A/C#   Cmaj7   E5/B
And I miss you so,   and I miss you so,
E5/D   A/C#   Cmaj7 E
Now you're gone I feel so alone, oh,   I miss you so.

| Am | Em | Am | Em ||

Verse 3

Amadd2   Emadd2
  I'd send you a flower, a sunflower bright
Amadd2   Emadd2
  'Cause you cloud my days, messing up my nights.
C   G
  And all the way up to the top of your head
F   Em
  Sun-shower kisses, I felt we had.

Chorus 2

       E5/D   A/C#   Cmaj7   E5/B
And I miss you so, oh baby I miss you so,
E5/D   A/C#   Cmaj7 E
Now you're gone I feel so alone,   oh, I miss you so, I do.

Instrumental ||: E | E | E | E | E   :||

Chorus 3   As Chorus 1

Outro

| E5/D | A/C# | Cmaj7 | E5/B |

E5/D   A/C#
All I gotta do is think of you,
Cmaj7   E5/B
  Oh, and I miss you so.
E5/D   A/C#
Baby, I'm afraid to say why,
Cmaj7   E
  Oh, and I miss you so.

| E5/D | A/C# | Cmaj7 | E5/B |

E5/D   A/C#
Baby, I'm afraid to say why,
Cmaj7   E
  Oh, and I miss you so.

Instrumental ||: E | E | E | E   :||

                    | E | E | E ||

LAYLA

Words & Music by Eric Clapton & Jim Gordon

Dm   B♭   C   C♯m7   G♯m7
D   E   E7   F♯m   B   A

Intro | N.C. | N.C. | N.C. | N.C. |
Guitar riff
| Dm B♭ | C Dm | Dm B♭ | C Dm |
| Dm B♭ | C Dm | Dm B♭ | C |

Verse 1
  C♯m7   G♯m7
What'll you do when you get lonely
  C♯m7   C   D   E   E7
And nobody's waiting by your side?
  F♯m   B   E   A
You been runnin' and hidin' much too long,
  F♯m   B   E
You know it's just your foolish pride.

Chorus 1
     A   Dm B♭
Layla, —
   C   Dm
Got me on my knees,
            B♭
Layla,
      C   Dm
I'm beggin' darlin' please,
            B♭
Layla,
   C   Dm   B♭ C
Darlin' won't you ease my worried mind?

© Copyright 1970, 1971 & 1998 Eric Clapton (25%)/Warner Chappell Music Limited,
Griffin House, 161 Hammersmith Road, London W6 (75%).
All Rights Reserved. International Copyright Secured.

Verse 2

C♯m7　　　　　　　　　G♯m7
Tried to give you consolation
C♯m7　　　　C　　D　　　E　　E7
When your old man let you down.
F♯m　　B　　E　　　　　　A
Like a fool, I fell in love with you,
F♯m　　　　　B　　　　　　　　E
You turned my whole world upside down.

Chorus 2

　　　A　　Dm　B♭
Layla, —
C　　　　　　Dm
Got me on my knees,
　　　　B♭
Layla,
　　C　　　　　　Dm
I'm beggin' darlin' please,
　　　　B♭
Layla,
C　　　　　　　Dm　　　　　　　B♭　C
Darlin' won't you ease my worried mind?

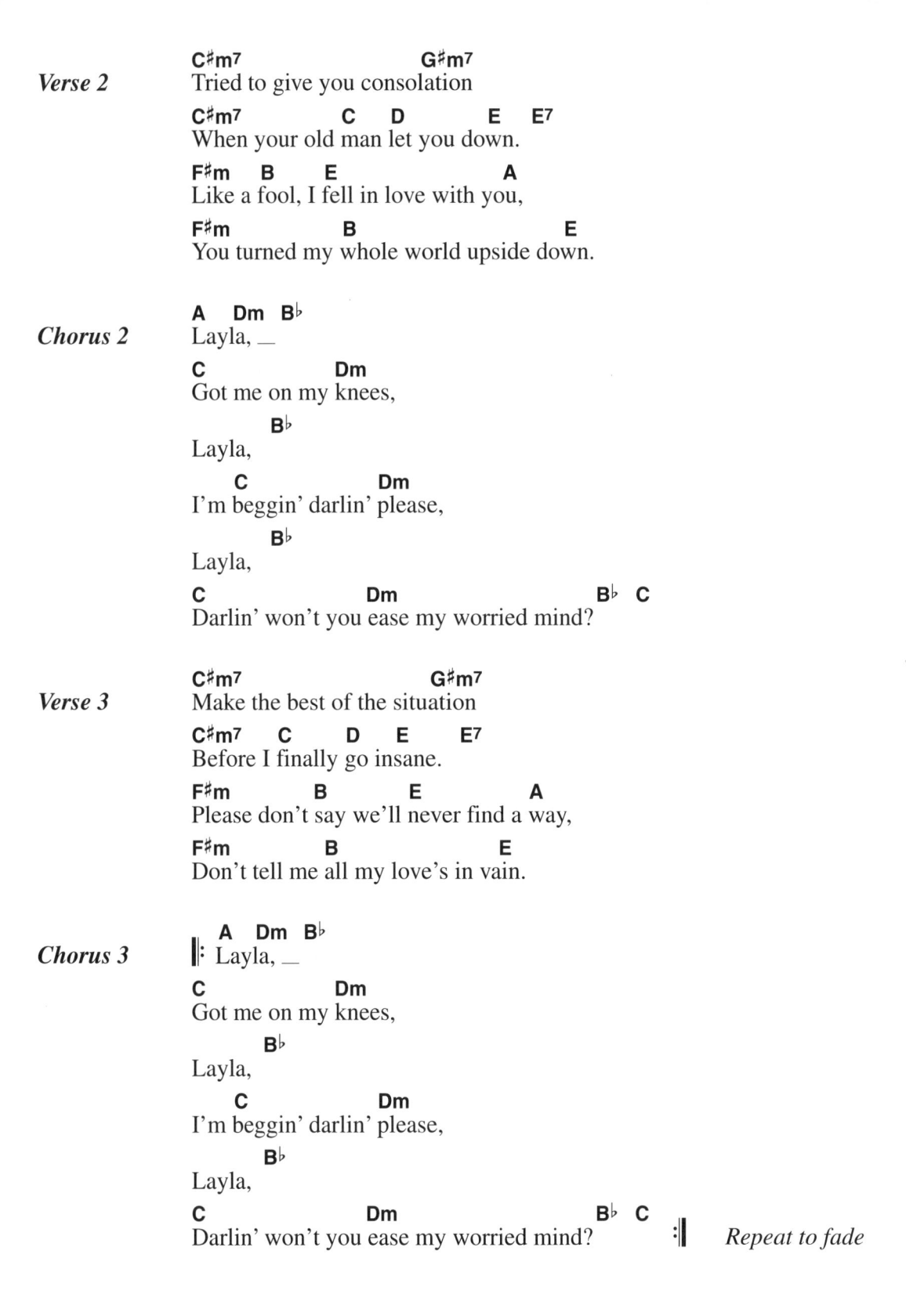

Verse 3

C♯m7　　　　　　　　　G♯m7
Make the best of the situation
C♯m7　　C　　D　　E　　E7
Before I finally go insane.
F♯m　　　　B　　　E　　　　　　A
Please don't say we'll never find a way,
F♯m　　　　　B　　　　　　　E
Don't tell me all my love's in vain.

Chorus 3

　　　A　　Dm　B♭
𝄆 Layla, —
C　　　　　　Dm
Got me on my knees,
　　　　B♭
Layla,
　　C　　　　　　Dm
I'm beggin' darlin' please,
　　　　B♭
Layla,
C　　　　　　　Dm　　　　　　　B♭　C
Darlin' won't you ease my worried mind? 𝄇　　*Repeat to fade*

SUNSHINE OF YOUR LOVE

Words & Music by Jack Bruce, Pete Brown & Eric Clapton

D   D7   F   G   G7   B♭   A   C

Intro | N.C. | N.C. | N.C. | N.C. |

| D D7 D | D   F D | D D7 D | D   F D ||

Verse 1
       D   D7 D   F D
It's getting near dawn
             D7 D   F D
When lights close their tired eyes,
        D7 D   F D
I'll soon be with you, my love
      D7 D   F D
Give you my dawn surprise.
     G G7 G   B♭ G
I'll be with you darlin' soon,
      G7 G   B♭ G
I'll be with you when the stars start falling.

Link | D D7 D | D   F D | D D7 D | D   F D ||

Chorus 1
  A   C   G
   I've been waiting so long,
  A   C   G
   To be where I'm going,
  A   C   G   A
   In the sunshine of your love. _____

Link | D D7 D | D   F D ||

Verse 2

         D   **D7 D**   **F D**
I'm with you my love,
                      D7 D   **F D**
The lights shining through on you.
                D7 D   **F D**
Yes, I'm with you my love,
                   D7 D   **F D**
It's the morning and just we two.
      G   **G7 G**   **B♭ G**
I'll stay with you darling now,
             G7 G   **B♭ G**
I'll stay with you 'til my seeds are dried up.

Link | D D7 D | D F D | D D7 D | D F D ||

Chorus 2   As Chorus 1

Solo | D D7 D | D F D | D D7 D | D F D | D D7 D | D F D |

           | D D7 D | D F D | G G7 G | G B♭ G | G G7 G | G B♭ G |

           | D D7 D | D F D | D D7 D | D F D | A | C G |

           | A | C G | A | C G | A | A ||

Link | D D7 D | D F D | D D7 D | D F D ||

Verse 3   As Verse 2

Link | D D7 D | D F D | D D7 D | D F D ||

Chorus 3

    A   **C**   **G**
  I've been waiting so long,
    A   **C**   **G**
  I've been waiting so long,
    A   **C**   **G**
  I've been waiting so long,
    A   **C**   **G**
  To be where I'm going,
    A   **C**   **G**   **A**
  In the sunshine of your love. _____ *Fade out*

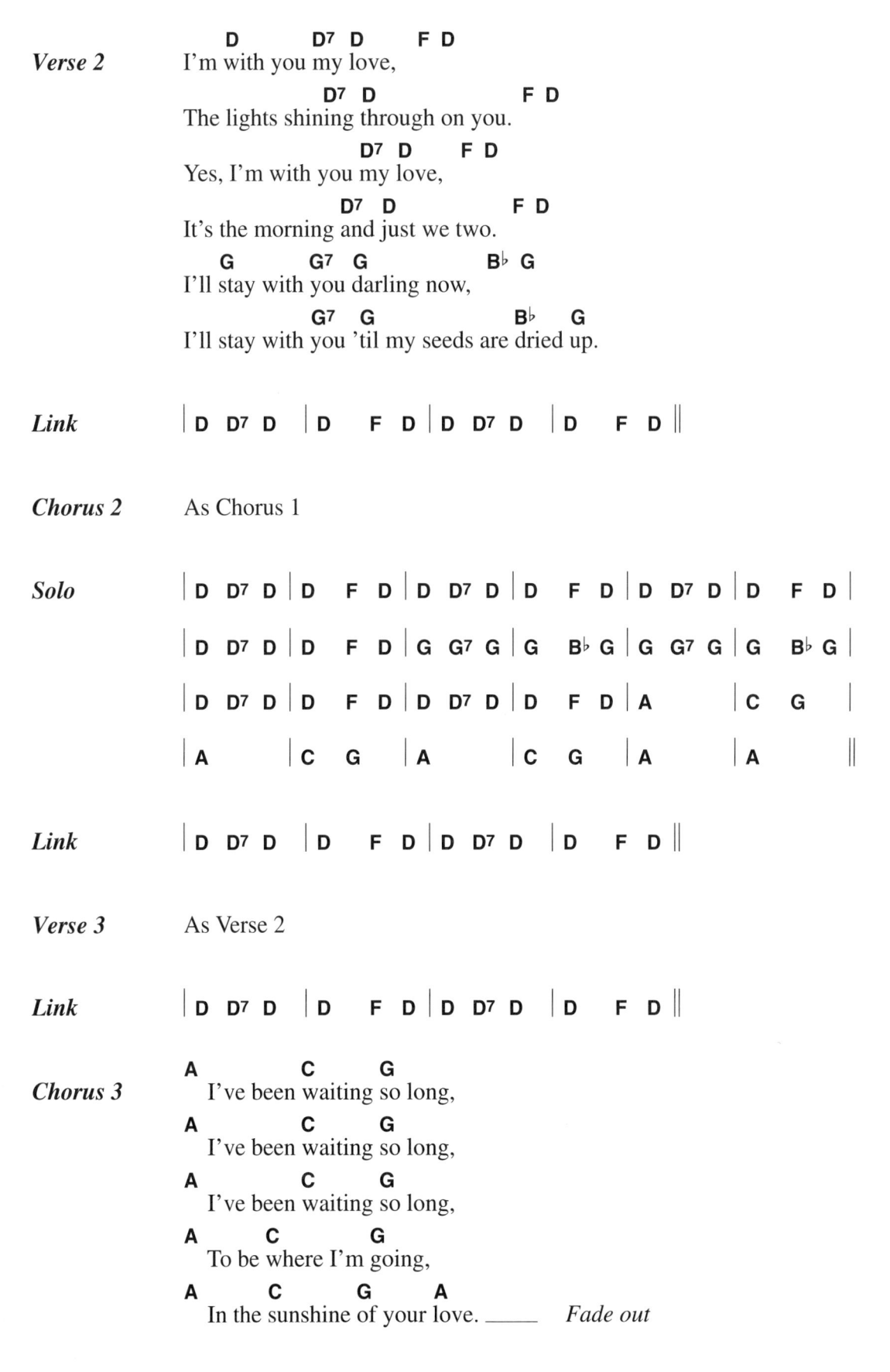

Tears in Heaven

Words & Music by Eric Clapton & Will Jennings

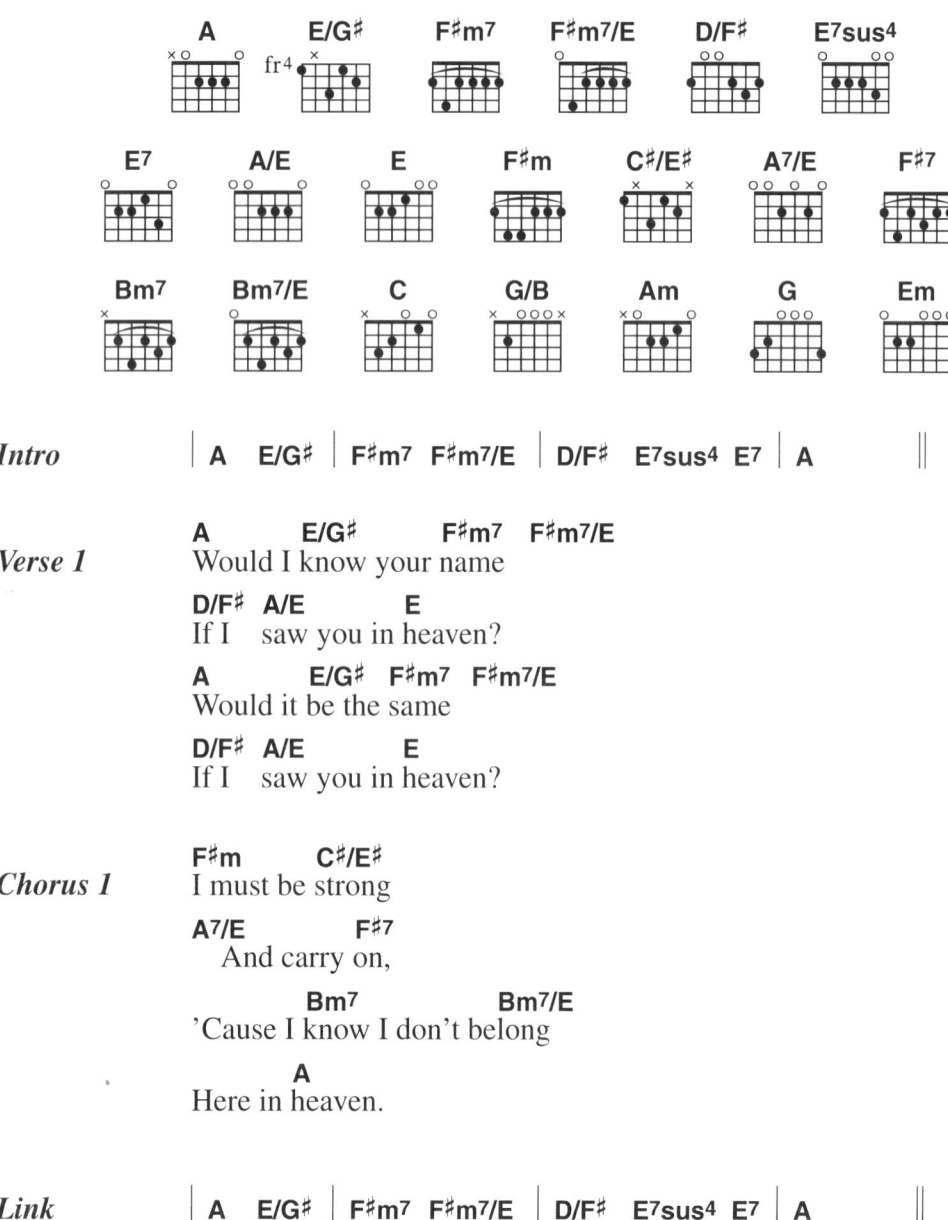

Intro | A E/G♯ | F♯m7 F♯m7/E | D/F♯ E7sus4 E7 | A ||

Verse 1

A　　　E/G♯　　F♯m7　F♯m7/E
Would I know your name

D/F♯　A/E　　　E
If I　saw you in heaven?

A　　　　E/G♯　F♯m7　F♯m7/E
Would it be the same

D/F♯　A/E　　　E
If I　saw you in heaven?

Chorus 1

F♯m　　C♯/E♯
I must be strong

A7/E　　　　F♯7
　And carry on,

　　　　Bm7　　　　　Bm7/E
'Cause I know I don't belong

　　　　A
Here in heaven.

Link | A E/G♯ | F♯m7 F♯m7/E | D/F♯ E7sus4 E7 | A ||

© Copyright 1991 & 1995 E.C. Music Limited, London NW1 (87.5%).
© Copyright 1991 Blue Sky Rider Songs administered by Rondor Music (London) Limited, 10a Parsons Green,
London SW6 for the World (excluding the USA & Canada) (12.5%).
All Rights Reserved. International Copyright Secured.

Verse 2

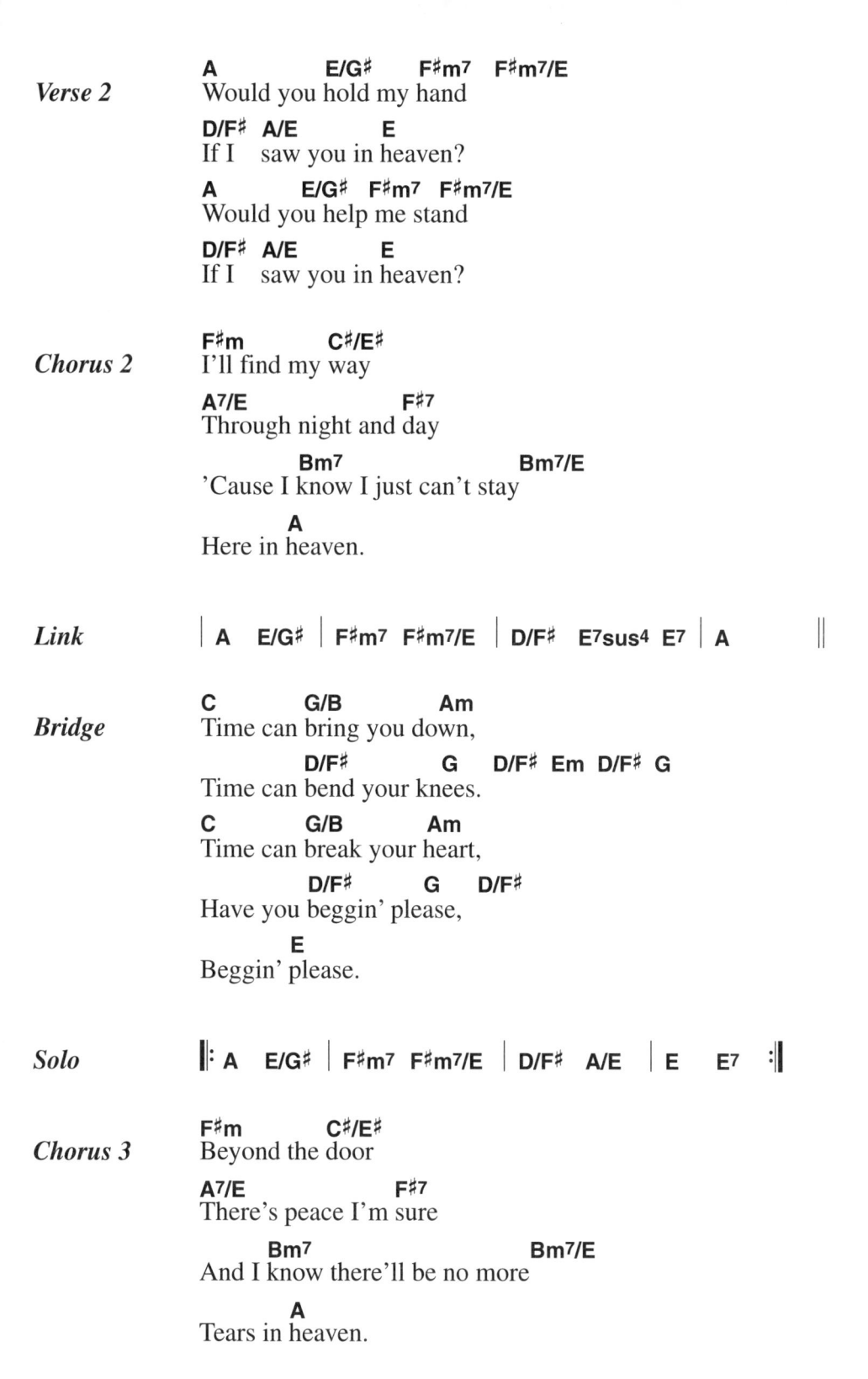

    A   E/G♯   F♯m7 F♯m7/E
Would you hold my hand

D/F♯ A/E   E
If I   saw you in heaven?

    A   E/G♯ F♯m7 F♯m7/E
Would you help me stand

D/F♯ A/E   E
If I   saw you in heaven?

Chorus 2

    F♯m   C♯/E♯
I'll find my way

A7/E   F♯7
Through night and day

        Bm7   Bm7/E
'Cause I know I just can't stay

      A
Here in heaven.

Link

| A E/G♯ | F♯m7 F♯m7/E | D/F♯ E7sus4 E7 | A ||

Bridge

  C   G/B   Am
Time can bring you down,

        D/F♯   G D/F♯ Em D/F♯ G
Time can bend your knees.

  C   G/B   Am
Time can break your heart,

        D/F♯   G   D/F♯
Have you beggin' please,

   E
Beggin' please.

Solo

|: A E/G♯ | F♯m7 F♯m7/E | D/F♯ A/E | E E7 :|

Chorus 3

    F♯m   C♯/E♯
Beyond the door

A7/E   F♯7
There's peace I'm sure

     Bm7   Bm7/E
And I know there'll be no more

    A
Tears in heaven.

47

Verse 3

```
         A        E/G♯     F♯m7   F♯m7/E
Would you know my name

D/F♯   A/E        E
If I   saw you in heaven?

A          E/G♯   F♯m7   F♯m7/E
Would you be the same

D/F♯   A/E        E
If I   saw you in heaven?
```

Chorus 4

```
F♯m        C♯/E♯
I must be strong

A7/E           F♯7
And carry on,

           Bm7           Bm7/E
'Cause I know I don't belong

           A
Here in heaven.
```

Link

| A   E/G♯ | F♯m7   F♯m7/E ||

```
           Bm7              Bm7/E
'Cause I know I don't belong

           A
Here in heaven.
```

Coda

| A   E/G♯ | F♯m7   F♯m7/E | A/E   E7sus4   E7 | A ||